A PAGE OF HISTOI

1944 to 1946

The striped blue-and-white illustration on the cover is taken from the writer's invitation to an ex-concentration camp internees' party held in "Gypsy Camp", Brunswick on 17th February 1946. Concentration camp internees wore blue-striped pyjama type clothing.

The other illustration is a photograph of the notice which appeared at the entrance to "Gypsy Camp", and is taken from the cover of the pamphlet 'Polish People in Germany', published by the Friends Relief Service, London in 1946.

The Team picture before departure

Back Row (left to right): *Bill B., Michael H., Lilian S., Hugh J., Marjorie A., Bill R., Eryl H.W.*
Front Row (left to right): *Joyce P., Kit B., Lilian I., Jane L., Beth C.*

A Page of History in Relief

LONDON · ANTWERP · BELSEN · BRUNSWICK

1944 to 1946

Compiled from a personal diary and letters,
with the assistance of
Friends Relief Service Team 100

by

Eryl Hall Williams

Sessions Book Trust
York, England

ISBN 1 85072 124 6

Printed by
William Sessions Limited
The Ebor Press, York, England

Preface

THIS LITTLE BOOK contains a personal account of the work of a Quaker Relief Team - RT100/FRS - in Europe in 1945 and 1946. The author was privileged to be a member of this Relief Team during the period from its formation in the autumn of 1944 up to June 1946. This account has been prepared with the co-operation of other surviving team members. Particular thanks are due to Beth Dearden (nee Clarkson), Hugh Jenkins, Jane Levy nee Levinson), and Joyce Parkinson, for their help and encouragement, and for contributing from their own recollections. Beth Dearden and Jane Levy have kindly contributed towards the cost of this publication, but the main cost has been shared between certain anonymous contributors, whose help is gratefully acknowledged and without which we should have been unable to proceed, and myself. I also acknowledge the great help and support of my wife and my sister-in-law, who have helped me with corrections and suggestions.

I wish my parents could have lived to see the use to which I put the letters home which I wrote so regularly and which they so diligently kept. This work should be dedicated to those who supported us in countless ways, material and financial, and to all those who care for the suffering of others less fortunately placed in our society.

I take full responsibility for any errors of fact and recollection. At this distance of time it is hard to be sure one has got it right but I have made every effort to record it as it was, with very little additional comment or interpretation. Let this page of history speak for itself!

ERYL HALL WILLIAMS

Contents

Illustrations

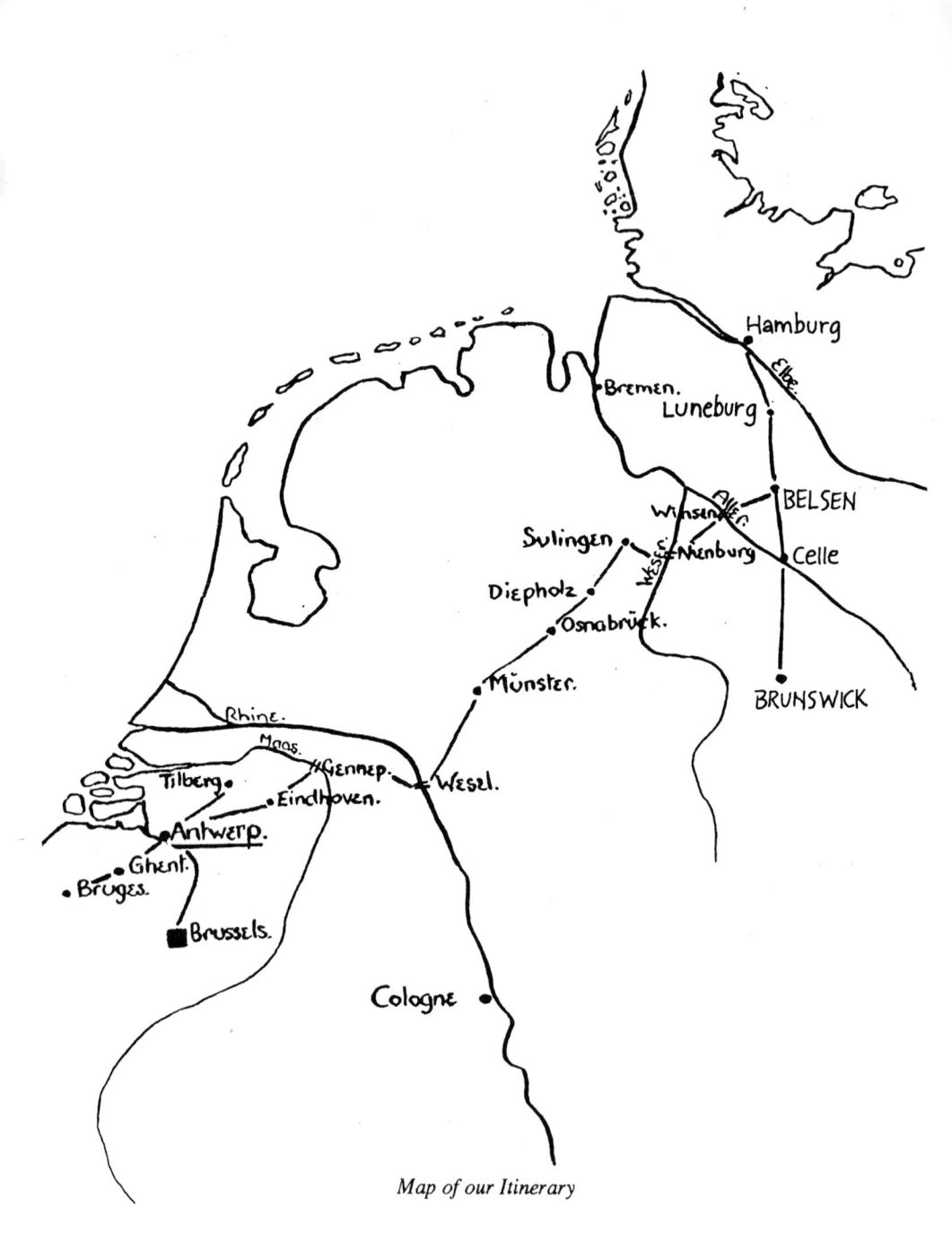

Map of our Itinerary

CHAPTER 1

Background and our time
in Antwerp

THE TIME WAS FEBRUARY 1945. World War II was coming to an end. We were waiting in Antwerp for a call to go to the aid of the Dutch population. We had recently crossed the English Channel in a tank landing craft from Tilbury to Ostend, after months of preparation in London. For a while we were stationed on the coast a little south of Ostend at Middlekerke, before being moved to Antwerp. The Allied invasion of Europe was progressing favourably after the Normandy landings of June 1944. While we were at Antwerp the war was still being fought along the valley of the Rhine. By the end of March 1945 a break-out was occurring from the bridgehead which had been achieved over the Rhine, and 21 Army Group was beginning to "crack about" in the plains of north Germany, to the east of the river crossing at Wesel, according to an Army newspaper. Eight bridges had been crossed and 11,000 prisoners taken. Further south, the American Army under the redoubtable General Patton had achieved similar Rhine crossings.

By the time we entered Germany and reached Belsen, the German armies were still holding out at Hamburg and Bremen, resistance continued to our right in the Ruhr and along the southern part of Bavaria, Berlin had not yet fallen but was surrounded, and pockets of resistance were still holding out at various points. On 19th April, 1945, The News Chronicle reported that armoured thrusts of British forces were only 17 or 18 miles to the south and south-east of Hamburg, and were advancing over a wide area of the Luneburg plain, while General Patton's American forces continued their advance in southern Germany.

1

Who were we? RT/100 - the Quaker Relief Team

There were twelve of us, drawn from a variety of backgrounds, who constituted the Quaker Relief Team RT/100, sometimes known as RS 100, or RT 11. We had assembled in London in the autumn of 1944 and trained for a few months in a large house in Hampstead, affectionately remembered as Mount Waltham, and later in Middlesex Street, London, in the City of London quite close to Liverpool Street Station and Petticoat Lane. An equal number of men and women, our ages ranged from barely twenty to about forty years of age. Some of us like myself had experience in the blitz in London doing social service work, and one was a trained nurse. Hugh was an experienced truck driver who as a conscientious objector had been driving produce to Covent Garden Market from farms in Surrey and Kent. Marjorie was a teacher of physical education, and rather jolly. She soon teamed up with our Team Leader, Lyn, who came from a Quaker county family in Essex and was resourceful and confident. Three, Jane, Beth and Joyce, were social workers with a variety of background and experience (one from Dr. Barnardo's). There was a married woman (Kit B.) with experience of catering, whose husband (Bill B.) was also a member of the Team. One was a Geordie shopkeeper/storeman (Bill R.) and another an aesthetic young academic type (the baby of the Team, Michael) who was planning to study at St. Andrews University, and eventually became a philosophy don at Oxford. I myself was just down from university in Wales, where I read law, and had been doing a variety of social work jobs as a condition of my being excused from military service as a conscientious objector.

An unlikely collection of souls you might think! We were part of a group of six Relief Teams assembled under the auspices of the British Red cross to prepare for the day when the Germans were expected to flood Holland on their retreat from their occupation. It was feared there would be millions of lives at risk of being drowned or starved and that disease would spread rapidly. The Army was primarily concerned with winning the war, but it was already making plans for the ensuing period of disruption, disorganisation and confusion, and SHAEF (Supreme Headquarters Allied Expeditionary Force) were eventually persuaded to accept the assistance of civilian relief teams under Red Cross co-ordination. On 11th December 1944 we were addressed by Charles Carter, a senior administrator at Friends House (he later became Vice-Chancellor of Lancaster University); he represented the Friends Relief Service in the negotiations. He described the situation which was anticipated in Holland as the German armies left. It was thought there would be three areas of flooding, 1) at the northern tip of the salient near Nijmegen; 2) across the belts of land south of Amsterdam; 3) through the southern sea walls near

Flushing (which was to be our concern). The Allies expected the Germans to evacuate Holland shortly, destroying the ports and flooding the countryside as they went. There was a Dutch Mission in SHAEF with Dutch personnel, and this was on stand-by in Belgium. The Civil Affairs Branch of the Army had trained Dutch civilians, but these were not sufficient, and help had been requested from the Red Cross and the Army. We would be responsible to both, and our status would be very definitely that of civilians, with no immediate responsibility to the military (a very important point for those like myself who were pacifists).

The scheme of work envisaged was that relief centres would be established in nine towns, to act as distribution centres for food supplies, to set up mobile hospitals and kitchens and to do relief work in general. Also to provide some relief for refugee workers by supplying mobile squads to render assistance where needed. About twenty specialists would be attached to the Civil Affairs Headquarters to advise on the general conduct of the work, including five doctors and five nurses, five refugee advisers, and five officers in command of relief teams. The Army hoped that these workers would eventually move into Germany after their work was done in about four months time, being attached to the Army to deal with displaced persons. Other voluntary societies taking part would include many Red Cross teams, five teams drawn from the Friends Ambulance Unit, four teams from the Salvation Army, and one or two teams to provide medical and general relief from the Scouts and Guides organisations. There would be one relief team and one medical team from Jewish Relief, and one medical team from Catholic relief, as well as one or two specialists drawn from the YWCA. A total of 23 relief teams would be involved, comprising no less than 700 persons. Later on a Spearhead group was formed, involving initially seven relief teams, three to be provided by the Red Cross, one by the Scouts, one by the Guides, one by the Salvation Army, and one by ourselves, the Friends Relief Service. In addition there would be two Hospital teams, one from the Red Cross and one provided jointly by the Guides and Scouts. There was talk of providing bath and laundry units to be manned by volunteers from Unilevers, the Red Cross and St. John's Ambulance. Add to this several individuals to act as Liaison Officers, administration officers, and one or two doctors, and the total would add up to 182 persons.

By this time the membership of the FRS team, which had fluctuated a little at first, became stabilised and we had assembled in London. We were to be accompanied by a doctor, Louis F., a splendid fellow whom I had known in the East End of London. Alas he never joined us, being denied his release from medical practice by the Ministry of Labour & National Service. Later

Training in London 1945
Field Kitchens in the garden of Mount Waltham

we learned that he had been drowned in a tragic swimming accident off the north coast of England. It was he who carried out the medical checks on us before we left, and gave us the necessary injections. (We had to attend the Burroughs/Wellcome laboratory in Bloomsbury for the tropical injections). The briefings and instruction continued for some months, and included practical exercises in outdoor cooking, and the assignment of roles to various members of the Teams was required by the authorities. I became the Clerk, Accountant, and Registration Officer, a role which led me eventually to assume responsibilities for the registration of displaced persons as they were received into our camp in Brunswick. We were issued a vast amount of equipment all of which had to be marked. There was some excitement when we went to collect our vehicles, consisting of two 15 cwt. Bedford trucks, two Austin four-berth ambulances, one 3-ton six wheel Austin truck, which had crawler gears. We had to paint out the khaki and substitute grey paint and add our Quaker star - which led to some confusion later on either with the German Army which wore grey uniform or the Allied invasion forces which used a Star marking. We were told that six drivers would be needed and that each must pass a War Office test. We made endless lists and had interminable meetings to discuss our plans.

The Friends Relief Service, as it was then called, had been formed in imitation of the Quaker effort in the first World War (Friends War Victims Relief) to provide organised relief services in case of need for the civilian population. Under the original name of Friends War Relief Service (F.W.R.S.), it had already carried out an extensive programme in connection with the evacuation of children from the large cities, and social service work in the East End of London, in Liverpool and other cities. Some members of our Team had taken part in such work, including myself. We were not paid but received our keep and pocket money which at the time we left Britain was nine shillings a week, plus a clothing allowance of a few shillings (which was not payable when we put on uniform). Members who were married received special allowances. As the end of the war approached, it was decided to merge the social side of the work of the Friends Ambulance Unit (F.A.U.) with the F.W.R.S. to form the Friends Relief Service, or F.R.S. for short.

The F.A.U. was different in that its members were prepared to don khaki uniform and engage in non-combatant duties in aid of the armed services, which we in the F.R.S. refused to do. Many of them eventually went to Greece as relief workers, and a colleague of mine at L.S.E., Huw R., another Welshman, served there for a while and tells tales of their adventures, some of which resemble the novel *Fortunes of War* for their bizarre quality, the strange turn of events, and the high spirits as well as the deep sense of futility which comes through.

The Team assembles in London, and departs for Ostend

In the autumn of 1944 the Team had been selected and assembled in a Victorian house in Hampstead, where we prepared for our mission, spending many months collecting our uniforms, vehicles and equipment, and impatiently awaiting our departure. A full account of this period appears in Appendix 1, "The Preparation in London and The Journey's Beginning". This includes an account of our departure and the voyage to Ostend.

My own background

I came from a family with a strong pacifist tradition on one side. My father had been a conscientious objector in the First World War, and suffered considerable hardship in consequence, being obliged to leave his job and seek refuge in a remote part of Wales for a while until it was safe for him to return to his home in Cardiff and resume his work in a housing association. A warrant was out for his arrest but it was never executed. He did appear before a tribunal, and received quite a warm commendation from the high-ranking military officer who presided for his transparent integrity. He rarely spoke about this period of his life, and it is only now when I read the papers he left that I can see what a hostile atmosphere he and his family must have encountered at that time.

When I became liable to military service, in 1941, I had no doubts about registering as a conscientious objector, and I went before three Tribunals before it was eventually settled that I could do 'humanitarian work'. At first I was allowed to continue my studies, but I had grave doubts whether I should do so. It was only when the Professor came to see me personally that I was persuaded that it would make a lot of sense to finish my studies before embarking on anything else. So I went back to College and completed my law degree in June 1942, after which I took up employment with the Welsh Y.M.C.A. based on Cardiff, where I was given the task of organising a Mobile Library Service for H.M. Forces. Serving different military bases where service men and women were situated, such as search-light and anti-aircraft batteries in remote areas, I visited these sites with my large Library van once a week to arrange for the lending of books. The work was not altogether to my liking, though the experience taught me something about military ways, and a little about driving large vehicles. I soon tired of my work as a Librarian, and applied to join the Friends War Relief Service

(F.W.R.S.). I was interviewed in East London and recruited to assist in the work of the Social Services section, based in Stepney, where I lived for a while in part of the medical students' hostel in Philpott Street, E.1, behind the London Hospital in Aldgate East. There we provided various daytime and evening social services in the locality to which were added firewatching duties which we performed regularly on a rota basis.

For some months I did Citizen's Advice Bureau work in Hackney under the kindly Mr. Lister and later on my own in Stoke Newington, also I helped with a youth club work in Wapping, at the Sugar Loaf public house. This had been damaged by bombing but repaired sufficiently to provide the base for a bunch of rowdy kids in a youth club, run by the immensely patient John H. This was the beginning of 'clubs for the unclubbable', which others like John Spencer and Merfyn Turner were pioneering elsewhere in Stepney in the form of the Barge Club. Prior to this, I did social casework for the Charity Organisation Society, a reputable charitable agency, from their office at Stepney Green. After training for a month I was given a regular case-load and made reports to the Committee and its hard-working Secretary Mr. Todd, (whom I later on encountered as an inspector in the Children's Department of the Home Office). The Committee met weekly to authorise grants of money to deserving cases. I cycled everywhere in Stepney, Limehouse and Poplar, and remember the rough cobbles only too well. I also remember the demands and the encouragement of the Secretary who closely supervised the case-work, and for some reason took a liking to me and my work and was strongly supportive. The Committee to which we presented our cases was somewhat intimidating and formal, being chaired by the awe-inspiring and sweet Lady W., who dressed all in black rather Edwardian ankle-length clothes, but who had a heart of gold, a clear mind, and deep dedication. Others included a leading local social service lady familiar with the area and a priest from the parish. It was rather a judgmental view which was taken of the merits of cases, I seem to remember, but I learned a good deal about human nature, on both sides of the table as it were.

I also learned about human nature on the night when fire-bombs rained on our street and the area where we lived was aglow. We made up a team to go to the nearby church which was alight, a fire bomb having lodged in one of the gutters between the gables. As we rushed down the aisle with our fire-buckets and stirrup pumps, once the caretaker had let us in, he shouted 'Be careful not to spill the water: the Church has been cleaned for tomorrow's service!'. Afterwards we put out smouldering fires in the upstairs room of a furrier whose workshop was on the first floor of one of the many tiny little one-up one-down Stepney terraced houses. When the air-raid was over, and

Bomb sites to allotments, Bethnal Green

the fire safely extinguished, the irate owner returned from the safety of the deep air raid shelter and berated us for soiling his precious fur skins with water!

For a short while I worked with some F.R.S. members on a bomb-site in Bethnal Green which we were clearing and preparing to convert into allotments. I didn't much care for the digging, but remember the thick marmalade sandwiches and mugs of tea we bought for our lunch in a local cafe. On one occasion I was taken down to see the underground station where F.R.S. was providing welfare services to those families who were camping out and sleeping all night on the platforms. I was asked if I was prepared to go and join the work there, but as I could not stand the heat, the general atmosphere, and the absence of fresh air, I politely but firmly declined to join the work there.

At the hostel we met in the evenings and at breakfast with other relief workers and exchanged experiences. I was particularly impressed by the two men in charge of organising our work, one John S., a solicitor who later went to work in Greece on relief work, and Dermot G., who after the War entered the prison service, and later became Governor of Oxford prison before retiring to Bristol, where, happily, he is still active in various good works, including the I.S.T.D. (The Institute for The Study & Treatment of Delinquency). He claims, not quite correctly, to have been my first employer! Then I remember the rather urbane Harry S., who went to Greece, two rather older men who were both solicitors with whom I had long chats, and the two persons who were in charge of the kitchen, Alan L. and Hannah W. (where in the day-time they were in charge of a cookery school for trainees). Alan and Hannah ran a tight ship, and sternly directed the cleaning of the kitchen by the orderlies each evening after dinner, which involved the requirement to scrub (not wash) the whole of the tiled area of the large kitchen, many square yards of red tile, also scrubbing the floors of the adjoining rooms such as the cold store and the vegetable room. We were very pleased when this back-breaking work on our knees was interrupted by an air-raid alarm, and we were allowed, sometimes hours later, on our return when the All-Clear siren had sounded, merely to mop the floor quickly before departing. Alan L. eventually entered the probation service, and I met him many years later in Stevenage.

Other duties performed on a rota basis included boiler duty, which involved tending and stoking the coke-fired boiler in the basement, which I never quite mastered, though others were deemed expert at this steamy chore. The trick was to avoid clinker forming at the base of the fire which had the effect of cooling the heat, yet allowing sufficient draught to make a hot fire and keep up the water temperature, which supplied the central-heating system and the baths, showers and wash basins, to an acceptable level. I seem to remember frequently producing a rather dead fire with abundant clinker, which my replacement would swear took him an hour to remove in order to get the fire back to a decent heat. I am sorry for those who wanted a hot bath in the meantime!

After my time in London I was posted to Liverpool, to work at the Friends Service Centre in Netherfield Road, Liverpool 5. This was one of the worst areas of the slums of Liverpool at the time; situated as it was not very far from the Liverpool docks, it had been heavily bombed. Anfield lay up the hill behind us but I never went to Anfield Road to see any football, only to the local Welsh chapel, whose minister and his wife were very welcoming and had a most charming daughter. Again the cycle was my means of transport, apart from the odd occasions when I went into town on one of the large lumbering 'green' goddesses' which passed the door. These were the Liverpool trams, which had the ability to steer by choosing tracks as they approached a set of points, and switching their course accordingly. I have frequently used the green goddess's ability to choose direction despite being a tram as a neat

Friends Service Centre, Liverpool

way of describing the choice we have remaining in our power even in a system which involves some pre-destination!

At the Friends Service Centre I found a small team of dedicated social service case-workers, who modelled themselves on the family case-work centres already pioneered by the Pacifist Service Units in Liverpool and various other urban centres, as well as using the established social service case-work methods, such as keeping meticulous case-records and having case-meetings to consider the best action to be taken on each case, and so on. Intensive family case-work had been well developed by this time, and David Jones, of the Liverpool P.S.U., was one of the prime movers. I later knew him as a member of the staff of the Mary Ward Centre in London, concerned with social work training, who eventually became its Principal. We were in friendly rivalry though not directly in competition.

One of the characters at our Centre was Alun D., a powerful thick-set and colourful Welshman who had a very loud booming voice, and whose sister had been in college with me. He had been studying electrical engineering in London at Imperial College before the war, and I had known his sister in college. He ran the workshop which renovated furniture for our clients situated above the shop where we interviewed clients and had our office. In his workshop he was assisted by one of our clients Bob, a rather slow-witted but willing young man who was unemployed because of his poor health. He became a disciple and devotee of Alun, as did we all, for the power of Alun's character was not limited to his voice and was too strong to be confined within his workshop and carried over to the rest of our lives. The head of the operation or Team Leader, as he was called, was Tom M., who had been a clerk in a brewery in somewhere like Burton-on-Trent in the Staffordshire potteries. A rather worried and anxious man, he was very sweet and patient. Frances was the cheerful and energetic cook-housekeeper. There were other members of the Team who came and went, and in due course after about a year and a half I too left, but not before I had made my mark by helping the Centre to survive a serious threat to its very existence.

Doubts had been cast on the value of the work and there was a threat to close it down. Faced with this, I conceived the idea that a professional consultant should be employed to prepare a report about the work of the Centre and advise about its future. This was done, and a lady from a University School of Social Work made a careful and independent study of the work and wrote a favourable report, with the result that the Centre survived, at least for the time being. By this time I was far away and immersed in my work in the East End of London, but I shall not easily forget those days in Liverpool. One summer we took a party of twenty or thirty boys for a week's holiday by the sea at Parkgate in the Wirral peninsula, and the days were full of hectic experiences running in bare feet over the mud flats to the sea, which at that time came right in to the shore only at high tide (nowadays it is gone forever!); coping with the injuries, indispositions, tantrums and moods of the boys and learning their bawdy songs from the slums. I also remember a weekend camp held in a hut on the shore at Formby. Vivid memories remain of the poverty and deprivation of some of the inhabitants of Liverpool who were our clients or 'cases'. For example, there was the elderly grandmother Mrs. S. who refused to move out of her basement two roomed flat, where the filth and squalor, the bed-bugs and fleas, the faded pictures and dirty bedclothes, combined to make each visit rather an ordeal. Our object was to persuade her to agree to being cleaned up and re-housed, but she was a very obstinate and determined old lady, who refused to budge. Her photograph appears in a book on the problems of the aged, which I still cherish. There were others too, like the work-shy youth who would not turn up for interviews with prospective employers, or who, when escorted there, and being offered a job, disappointed everyone within days by not getting up in the morning in time to present himself for work. There was the plausible Irish rogue with his co-habitee and large family who ran up huge rent arrears and debts and defeated the system by twisting it to his advantage at every point, freely telling lies and with a gift of the gab of which any Irishman would be proud. We used to stand in the bath after some of these visits and strip off to get rid of the fleas!

An account of the work of The Friends Service Centre has been published separately by The Ebor Press.

Our time in Middlekerke

On our arrival in Ostend my diary recounts my various meetings with an old school friend, Stanley Smith, who was in the RAF, and whom I had spotted standing on the steps of the services club in Ostend as we drove by on the road south. He had seen me and found out where we were billeted, so we had many happy times together, and a few ice creams and cups of tea. My diary's first entry concerns the day we arrived in Ostend, and reads as follows:-

> **February 28 1945**
> It was with very little hope of seeing him that I looked out for Stanley as we drove through the streets in our snaking convoy. I asked the passengers to look out for any RAF boys and suddenly they pointed out a group. At this instant I noticed Stanley on the corner outside an RAF hotel. We all waved; could not stop; and passed on thinking he had not seen me. Arrived at M. in the early afternoon, famishing. Had a poor meal. Staying in 3 hotels, Astoria - Red Cross; Melrose (where we feed) - Scouts and Guides; Pension Julia Simonne - Quakers and Salvation Army. Michael and I share a bed and bedroom. H & C & a view over the town as we are on the top floor. Madame is very talkative & tells us about the occupation. It is the first time she has had "the Army" billeted on her, and now she will have some coal. Night guards have to be mounted on the vehicles, which are on the promenade.

Our billet was a vacant seaside boarding house in Middlekerke a few miles south of Ostend, where we learned from our landlady something of the experiences of the German occupation. We had to mount guard on our vehicles at night (in shifts) and it was sometimes very cold and miserable. During the next few days we had various briefings about such matters as Security, Censorship, Facilities, and Gerald Gardiner (head of the Friends Ambulance Unit, whom we had met in London) came on Wednesday, February 28th and talked to us about the history of the Friends Ambulance Unit. We had a map-reading lesson, did some motor vehicle maintenance, a Civil Affairs brigadier spoke to us words of welcome and encouragement at a a parade in a windy street, to which we had repaired, thankfully without having to march, though it seems the Guides did actually march there! We went so far as self-consciously to line up 'soldier-fashion', my diary records. The brigadier said it took a great load off their minds to know that we were now available - he was glad to see that our party included 'the Friends'. It seems he knew a rather weighty Friend called Bertha Bracey. We took time off for various expeditions, achieved by hitch-hiking, such as a day trip to Bruges. We went to the pictures and saw Claudette Colbert in an old film, after tea at the Officers' Mess in Ostend, a look around the shops, and dinner. Later I saw the film 'No, No, Nanette!' with Anna Neagle. The film broke down at an intriguing spot, and we had a 20 minutes break while everyone consumed a vast ice-cream costing 10 francs. Another film I saw at this time was 'Pimpernel Smith'.

We had talks about disinfestation, about dealing with D.P.s (the abbreviation we had learned for Displaced Persons), Sanitation and First Aid. Eventually the time came for us to move and we knew that a move was imminent. At first it was rumoured that we were to go to a city to engage in what was described as 'civil defence'. This set the alarm bells ringing with the pacifist members of our Team (including myself). We made it clear that we had not come out here to do a Civil Defence job. There were rumblings and deep and anxious discussions took place. On the very eve of our departure my overcoat which had been torn on one of our hitch-hiking expeditions was returned duly mended in exchange for two bars of soap - which on the black market were said to sell for 30 francs each or 3/6d. The next day the Salvation Army, Scouts and Guides Teams left smoothly. Our departure was imminent, so Mike and I hitched a lift into Ostend, had tea and dinner at the Officers' Mess and an ice-cream in between. There we learned that we too were off in the morning, so we hurried back, and were on night watch for two hours that night, worst luck! Our duty was from 4 a.m. to 6 a.m. after which we loaded the vehicles and took breakfast, setting off later with 20 vehicles in all (4 Teams).

The Movement Order we received was to move from our base on the coast near Ostend, Middlekerke, to Antwerp. The Movement Order was as follows:-

ITINERARY FOR CONVOY NO. 2   RT/11/FRS
Slype - St. Pierre Cappelle - Ghistelles, slap across.
Roxem, follow main road. Branch right at Aeltre.
South to Leetenhulls. Vynckt. Deynze, bear left to Deurle.
Just before level crossing look for M.P.s (Military Police) Ghent. Escort to Antwerp road number 200. Enter Antwerp through tunnel into Canal du

Brasseur - turn right into Avenue d'Italie which continues into Avenue de France.
Destination, Antwerp.

We travelled through country which became progressively more interesting, with large farmsteads, quaint pyramid-roofed barns, some woodland and even an occasional rise! Part of our route lay along a modern two track road, (we would call it a motorway today but we did not know that description then) which seemed fairly new, with clover leaf crossings. We picked up the Military Police (M.P.s) to take us through Ghent, and arrived at our destination about 3.30 p.m. We drove through a tunnel under the river Scheldt and parked outside the Civil Affairs offices in some public gardens. Then a long wait while night arrangements were made: we were 24 hours too soon for the Army, it seems! The women went to a Church Army hostel, four men (including Michael and myself) were posted to guard our vehicles in the grounds of a blitzed Jesuit College, St. Joseph's Seminary, the rest of the men went to a four-star hotel, the Century Hotel, a grand modern establishment in the centre of the city. Michael and I dined at the Officers' Mess and were treated royally by Colonel C. and Major O. That evening a little boy showed us round the College. We saw rats in the courtyard. The next night Michael, Hugh and I enjoyed the fleshpots while the others stood guard in the vehicles.

Our time in Antwerp

Together in Antwerp, as we had been for a short while in London, we found ourselves messing in the Infants School situated in the back streets of an old part of Antwerp (or should one say, messing about together), waiting for a summons to do something useful, as my diary entries explain. We practised our Dutch, which was not yet at a very advanced level, cleaned and checked our vehicles and equipment, had endless Team Meetings around the sand-pit in the yard, visited the city and neighbouring towns on brief and sometimes rather extravagant excursions, and waited. At night we were frequently awakened by the sound of the V1s and V2s (the guided rocket weapons which had been developed by this time by the Germans and were being fired from German bases at Peenemunde in North Holland). The Germans were now aiming these at the city and port of Antwerp, having given up trying to get them through to London because radar had enabled so many to be intercepted. The echo of the explosions shattered our peace as we tried to sleep in the classrooms. Somehow the corridors acted as a sounding-box, and we swore the bombs were entering at one end of the corridor and going out at the other

Antwerp, the infants' school yard at Merksem

end! Otherwise we were not unduly concerned about the bombing, as most of us had been through the Blitz in London or elsewhere!

After arriving in Antwerp and spending the first night dispersed in various locations, including a first-class hotel for those who were lucky in the draw, the next day the Team had reassembled in the rather dirty courtyard of the Jesuit College. We made our lunch, using petrol cookers (possibly for the first time since our exercise days in Hampstead and the last time too - they were so dangerous to use!), a soya boiler, and an incinerator. All were put to good use, and in the evening we enjoyed a first-class meal, which was largely Kit's work. All the vehicles went to fill up with petrol, and we waited while our team Leader Lyn was negotiating all day with the Civil Affairs officers and arranging our work. Rumour was that the four teams would work in four outlying districts of Antwerp, ourselves in Merksem, where, thankfully, we would do more welfare work than first aid.

The next day we moved to the Infants School in Merksem, Antwerp, Violetstraat. The toilets and washbasins were very low, which caused some amusement! It was a large nursery school built on an L-pattern, with spacious classroom, a resident caretaker, electricity and above all an enclosed courtyard where we could park our vehicles without supervision which was great! After our arrival we spent the day cleaning our vehicles, unpacking and setting up our kitchen, living room and dining room, and bedrooms. There followed an interesting Team Meeting when Lyn gave us a report on her activities since our arrival in the city. A full programme of ambulance work, rest centre work, FAP (First Aid Post) and shelter work was envisaged. We set to work assembling some pre-fabricated furniture which Hugh had collected from the municipality, and had a good meal in the evening. There were several bombs in the night.

By this time arrangements had been made for local people to do our laundry and help as vegetable orderlies and with the cooking and cleaning. Lyn had contacted the FAU unit in Antwerp and we found them very helpful. Two of their members, Bill P. and Duncan J., came over to visit us. Beth and I went exploring in Merksem, and visited two shelters situated in dockside factories, where the Civil Affairs Major wanted us to start shelter work. At the subsequent Team Meeting it was revealed that we were now expected to set up a Rest Centre in the Kindergarten at Violetstraat and do the ambulance job, but to soft-pedal the shelter work because we might not be there more than a few days longer. We had some discussion about how to adapt the premises for a Rest Centre.

The following day a representative of COBSRA (the Council of British Societies for Relief Abroad) Miss R. arrived with our mail and cash and brought news of the other Teams. She was seconded from the YWCA and was responsible for the non-Red Cross Teams in our group. She was accompanied by Miss B., a very senior Red Cross representative whom we knew from the time of our assembly in London. We were also subjected to a brief visit of inspection from Colonel A. (British Red Cross Commission commandant) and Colonel C. (Civil Affairs), who made a cursory inspection of the premises.

One afternoon Michael and I set off in his Bedford to explore our assigned ambulance district. We broke down on the way back from Schoten to Merksem, and I hitched a lift part of the way and walked back the rest to fetch help. Hugh and I took the big Austin six-wheeler truck to tow Michael home. When we pulled up suddenly Michael crashed into our rear and smashed his radiator. In the evening we discussed a useful plan produced by Jane for turning this place into a hostel for those rendered homeless by the bombing, in particular the aged or infirm.

There is a story about Michael on this occasion. He was the youngest member of the Team, and quite a scholarly fellow, who rather fancied his linguistic ability and thought he would try it out when he could. Driving back into our yard after this breakdown, he saw two small boys and greeted them in what he thought was Flemish. Apparently they rushed off to tell their mother they could understand English! Although we wore those grey uniforms, we were still easily recognisable as a British contingent, it seems.

We received some hospitality from the Borough Furniture Officer, the kindly Monsieur V. He showed five of us round the city, including some houses which he had designed (for he was a bit of an architect) and invited us to his house for tea, where we met his charming wife and a married daughter who had artistic interests. He regaled us with stories of the suffering during the occupation, the rubbery textured bread, and the liberation and the time when he and his wife were trapped in the cross-fire between the retreating German Army and the liberating armies for several hours near his home. Rations were now improving but a black market was flourishing. We also entertained several FAU members for dinner, one who had visited five FAU sections, some already in Germany and the rest about to move there. He spoke of the difficulties they had experienced with the military and of the behaviour of British troops which was causing some concern.

At this time we heard reports of a camp of 20,000 persons somewhere in Germany where the FAU were having to be very careful and correct in their behaviour while around them people were starving, with one meal a day, one blanket and sleeping on straw. We wondered whether it might be possible for us as the FRS Team to go there for a while pending our imminent assignment to Holland. A month there might make all the difference. We later were informed that the British authorities had an agreement with the Russians not to allow any voluntary societies to work in Germany, and that the position of the FAU was so delicate that no further steps should be taken, but Lyn promised to have a word with Gerald Gardiner, who was the General Secretary of the FAU at this time (he later became Lord Chancellor).

Jane and Lyn gave us a report of their visit to a school at Merksem which they had chosen for a Rest Centre. The local Burgermeister was co-operating, a team of workers was busy clearing, cleaning, and installing furniture, and it all seemed very satisfactory. Two local people would run the Centre, and one or two members of our Team would spend 24 hours at a time there for a start. Meanwhile the scheme for an old people's hostel at Violetstraat had been scrapped, but there was some talk of helping in a clothing distribution. Lyn had contacted an officer who worked in the Returned Vehicle Park and arranged to collect many oddments for the vehicles - we hope to get authority for tyres', according to my diary.

Another day Miss R. arrived bearing mail (eight letters for me) and newspapers. We learned that plans were afoot for moving our headquarters to

Holland immediately. The situation there was desperate, with people having to survive on no more than 320 calories a day, one tenth of what the League of Nations had estimated to be a person's normal needs. The Salvation Army team were clearing a village of scabies and impetigo, the Scouts were working with refugees, the Guides with D.P.s (Russians and Poles). We were glad to be so near at hand and prayed for the opportunity to assist these stricken people.

Meanwhile the waiting continued. It was now nearing the end of March and we had achieved very little. We took the opportunity when we were 'off duty' to visit neighbouring teams and renew our acquaintance with some of their members. But clearly our impatience was growing. Nearly a month more was to pass before we received our orders to move.

One day I went to fetch the rations and NAAFI goods. The former were held in a vast warehouse and I was interested to see all the trucks from different units queuing up. At the NAAFI they were surprised that we took none of our 1000 cigarettes or any spirits except one bottle of whisky (for colds). Our abstinence was not to last under the trying circumstances we encountered later!

On March 25th, Sunday, the diary reads:

> Quiet morning writing letters. Monsieur V., wife and grandson to lunch, also Miss D. of Red Cross Hospital & F. I got a lift with them to the Hospital at Schilde. Joyce with me. After looking round their chateau, which is surrounded by a moat, and is set in lovely woodlands, we walked to G.'s place. Team 105 are in one wing of a Monastery run by the White Fathers, an Order with African and East Indian connections. Tea with Miss W., G., B. and K. Hitched back. I retired early to bed with a distended stomach. A noisy night but I heard little of it. V1's said to have cut out in the courtyard. News of great offensive over the Rhine - & Churchill over as well! We are now on 24 hours' call to move.

On March 27th 1945 my diary records that the Allies had crossed the Rhine the previous weekend and Montgomery's troops were pushing into the Ruhr. 'How much longer will we have to wait?', the entry asks. The 'things that go bump in the night' had ceased for many nights now. A little later, on April 1st 1945, we heard on the radio that the Germans were evacuating North Holland. This led to much speculation about our future. Will we go there and will there be flooding? Or will we be diverted to Germany?

On one occasion we entertained to supper a padre from Wesley House and his assistant, Leslie F. and Bob M. They promised to try to help us get a parcel to our fellow workers in Paris, who are short of food, comforts, matches etc. 'Things must be very tight for them as they are not on Army rations', I remarked.

By April 4th we were on 48 hours' call to move. Four of us went one day in a Bedford truck to Brussels, where we lunched with several FAU members. I visited Mary Trevelyan who was at the YMCA Leave Hostel and formerly worked with the Student Christian Movement (S.C.M.) in which I had been active as a student. She told me how difficult it had been to make contact with S.C.M. people on her visits to Holland and France. She had been to Paris. Miss R. (Red Cross) explained that after our move to Holland we would be grouped in "concentration areas", and that 200 British medical students may be coming. She showed us poignant letters from the Burgermeisters of many Dutch towns, which had been received via the International Red Cross. They described the possible consequences of the present conditions as "catastrophic"!

On Sunday, April 8th, Lyn phoned from the Civil Affairs to say we were going on Tuesday a.m. On Monday afternoon we were told by Lyn to indent for normal rations, in other words, we were not moving after all! The diary records "Chagrine, much gnashing of teeth, all very fed up. Sat about in the sun commiserating". Joyce's diary reveals that we were expecting to move at any minute, and this affected the work at the Rest Centres, which sadly had to be handed over to the local people. During the next few days, Lyn and Hugh went to Tilburg to see Miss R. while Joyce, Bill and Kit went with them as far as Rosendaal to help the Salvation Army on scabies clean-up. They reported the most terrible cases of scabies with complications - impetigo, carbuncles, also signs of malnutrition - an old man with skin like a deflated balloon, crinkled and hanging off his shoulders (we were to see plenty more like this later) - and children with pot bellies. After some weeks in Antwerp the call came, but it was not after all to go to Holland. Thankfully Hitler had not after all ordered the dykes to be opened and the civilian population of the Netherlands was saved from drowning, though they did experience extreme hardship including food shortages. We were ordered to proceed at the greatest possible speed to Northern Germany, where a Concentration Camp had been liberated and our help was more desperately needed.

CHAPTER 2

The Journey to Belsen

THE MOVEMENT ORDER we received was as follows:

18th APRIL, 1945

CA 648. SECRET. MOVEMENT ORDER. You will move Thursday 19th April. ETD 0.600 hrs. Stage night 19/20 204 CA Det KEVELAER. ETA 2 British Army Main Hqs 18 hrs 20 April. Present location 2 British Army Main Hqs BORSTEL MR W 844545 nr SIEDENBURG. Final destination BELSEN Concentration Camp. Four days rations to be carried. Route 2 Army Main Axis.

My photograph album bears the inscription under a photograph of the Team's vehicles being overtaken by a farm cart:

'On the road to who knows what? In Holland, 19th April 1945, we stop by the roadside on the way to Kevelaer (which was to be our first night stop) (Engine trouble).'

When we arrived at Kevelaer there was nowhere for us to stay except at a small Convent, where the nuns were very welcoming but we, the men, had to sleep in our vehicles in the courtyard. Again there were rats in the courtyard.

The next page of the album reads rather pompously:

"We drove through history, a few days or weeks after the advancing armies. We passed through many Dutch villages and German towns and villages which had been devastated. We were appalled - but drove on - for 3 long days, stopping the night at Kevelaer and Sulingen, bei Diepholz" (to which we were to return briefly later, after we left Belsen).

On the road to Germany, outside Kevelaer

A newspaper cutting dated 29th April 1945 with a map of the front shows that the war was still on, though we ourselves had very little news - not knowing where the front was. When we did our historic drive, Bremen and Hamburg were still holding out, Berlin had not fallen, and there was still resistance to our right in the Ruhr.

We crossed the Rhine on a Bailey Bridge known as the Montgomery Bridge at Xanten to which we gained access by precariously swinging our vehicles off the road and down the bank of the river, with Military Police waving frantically to the drivers to keep going in case we got stuck in the mud. We passed through the devastated towns of Munster and Osnabruck, where the scene of destruction was total, and such as one can hardly find words to describe. All street names were gone and the road wound its way through rubble, from which one could occasionally discern some item of familiar domestic use such as a kettle or a child's doll.

RT/100 arrived at Belsen on April 21st 1945, just six days after the first British Army Unit and the day the evacuation of the sick from the camp by the RAMC began.

The Allies had imposed a 'non-fraternisation order' regarding relations with the Germans. This was already in force as we entered Germany, and my photograph album contains an account of the concern felt at Yearly Meeting of the Society of Friends (the Quaker religion's governing body) held that year at the headquarters of the Society of Friends in London about the implications for relief teams. In fact two teams were held up while the matter was being considered. It seems that the Society of Friends could not bind itself or those working under its auspices to obey such an order. Roger Wilson's book *Quaker Relief* (1952) describes vividly the anxious debate which took place about this issue. But we were already in Germany, and the album says that we would not have been prevented from answering the call to Belsen by this development, nor, as I recall, were we greatly hampered by it in the ensuing days and months. There were times, however, during the early part of our stay in Braunschweig (Brunswick), to which we went after Belsen, when it proved slightly embarrassing not to be able to reciprocate the kindness shown to us by various German families.

CHAPTER 3

The Work at Belsen (clearing the Camp, Hospitalisation & Welfare

THIS CONCENTRATION CAMP was uncovered in peculiar circumstances. It was handed over to the British under a truce arranged at the request of the German authorities, as they feared that the internees would escape and spread typhus all over the countryside. The British insisted on keeping the Commandant and S.S. men responsible for the brutalities in the camp. The S.S. were at first put to work burying the thousands of dead, and those who survived this were to have been sent to stand their trial. Under the same truce, Hungarian soldiers continued to guard the camp.

The camp lay between Hannover and Hamburg, slightly nearer Hannover, and not very far from the town of Celle, in the middle of the Luneburg Heath. Hamburg was just over 100 kilometres to the north, and Hannover just over fifty kilometres to the south-west. The area is fairly flat, wooded and entirely agricultural; it is very beautiful country. The dark pine woods are bordered by silver birches, the roads are lined by cherry trees, there is an air of peace and serenity which at times made it impossible to believe that the gruesome tragedies in the camps were anything but a night-mare. The camp was surrounded by a harmless looking wire fence, and the barbed and electrified fences which surrounded the concentration camp proper were several yards inside this fence, and not easily visible from the road. It seemed extremely likely that the peasant and farmer population living in the villages which surrounded the camp on every side were not fully aware of what was going on inside the camp; they were an uncurious people, and it might have been difficult for them to know how bad the conditions there were, though no doubt they may have had their suspicions.

The burning of the huts, Belsen, May 1945

There were really four adjacent camps; Camp number 1 was the Concentration camp, and it had been built, so we were told, as a prisoner-of-war camp for a few thousand people. (Some Russian prisoners-of-war were quartered not very far off.) The sanitary arrangements might have been adequate for this purpose, but housing eventually so many people, (and it had been used for seven months before our arrival as a Concentration Camp), the sanitary arrangements soon became totally inadequate, and as no steps were taken to improve them, they became foul and were never used. Water was then obtained from stagnant reservoirs, and even in quantity was totally inadequate for drinking and/or washing; the ground and the floors of the huts were used as lavatories. As many as 1,000 people were living in huts intended for 60 prisoners, and indeed it was said that the German authorities intended to house as many as 50,000 in them. The internees were all verminous; not as we generally know vermin in England, but so that they picked off handfuls of louse whenever they felt like it. Typhus was the predominant illness; tuberculosis was very prevalent, there was some typhoid, some diphtheria, much dysentery, and a wide variety of bad skin diseases, including extremely bad sores and abscesses. Soup and bread had been the diet for about six months, but during the last three weeks before the arrival of the British, it seems that swede soup, and later raw swedes, was the only food

24

which the internees received. Hundreds of people died every day in the grounds of the camp, hundreds of others died in the huts; in some cases, the living were able to drag the dead out of their huts and leave them on the ground; in other huts, the living were themselves so weak that they had to remain with the dead amongst them, the numbers increasing daily.

An eye-witness account written at the time of liberation by one Dr. Fritz Leo, a medical doctor who had been one of the camp's internees, and authenticated by eight other doctors who were at one time or other detained there as internees, explains how the Belsen Camp had been intended by the S.S. as a medical camp. Instead of simply exterminating the sick and the frail, as had been their practice hitherto, they decided to transport them to Belsen from other camps such as Sachsenhausen, and some of the doctors arrived with high hopes of finding improved conditions. They were to be sadly disappointed. [Rudi Kustermeier's account seems to confirm this: see Appendix 2].

"In pouring rain, our long column drew out of the station on to the long road; and in the rain we stood for a long time, waiting in front of the poverty-stricken, tumbledown wooden huts which were to be our new home. So that was the hospital camp! Several 50-metre long huts, without the least interior fittings. Through the leaky roof the rain dripped, making great pools inside. A few bundles of straw lay here and there on the earth, mainly half wet. In parts, doors and windows were missing and through the openings and the cracks whistled the cold wind. Packed together like sardines - 7-800 men were squeezed into each hut. In the first days there was still bread, although very little, and there was also a thin, watery swede soup which the people devoured with great eagerness. But the straw was soon so wet that it was unusable and all were lying on the bare wooden boards..."

"For the thousands of people who were already there, there was in those first days no possibility of treatment. Patients with fever, open tuberculosis, cripples, people with great wounds, all lay on the ground. Neither medicaments nor dressings nor anything for the treatment of the sick was placed at our disposal... every morning there was a roll-call which usually lasted 3-4 hours and often much longer. In the freezing cold, in rain and wind, everyone stood and shivered, morning after morning, until the many thousands had been counted. Many collapsed every day, never to stand up again. The weak ones were dragged into a special block, the notorious block 15, where they slowly but surely perished. At one end of this block was the big mortuary, and in front of it, in the hall, lay those who were already dead; in front of those, the half-dead and the dying, and in front of them those who were not yet dead. It was a ghastly downward progression...:"

Dr. Leo describes how, after a while, three small huts were placed at their disposal as medical people to act as a sick bay. Apart from much filth and rubbish, there was nothing inside at all. But standing outside were some rickety, broken wooden beds. The doctors and some male nurses cleared out the filth and carried in and repaired the wooden beds, so that eventually some small rooms were available for patients. Then they acquired a few drugs, but they were not in a position to take into the sick-bay more than 400 of the many thousands who were sick and needed treatment. Even this number was achieved only by putting two men in each bed, "if one could call them beds. They were only wooden frames, with a couple of blankets, no straw, no mattresses, no sheets, we had not even towels for the patients. And there, on the bare boards of the frames, lay these creatures, mostly reduced to absolute skeletons by hunger."

"There was seldom any water. For many days it was cut off, and we needed cleaning facilities so badly... Bread became shorter and shorter and finally there was none at all for many days. The people were packed like flies, and we had several hundred dead every day, and on several days more than a thousand."

"And then the notion occurred to the S.S. to dispatch from all the Concentration Camps in Germany, to the hospital-camp at Bergen-Belsen, the people who were too weak and ill and worn out with work. Then they came in great transports, often numbering several thousand people, mostly by rail, 70-100 to a truck, penned in together for several days on end, often without food or drink. They were transferred into trucks and then staggered out into the camp. Mostly there were already hundreds dead and already green with corruption. Among the living there were many who could no longer walk, in fact not even crawl. They filled our camp once again with thousands of people in need of help, and our means were so infinitesimal!"

In March 1945, according to this testimony, the S.S. decided to build a gas chamber at Bergen-Belsen, half underground. The plans were prepared and the workmen commissioned by the time the British arrived. By this time there were piles of corpses in front of all the huts and beside them, lying piled up in heaps, all naked, many green and rotting. The clothing was burned separately. A small crematorium at one end of the camp was working day and night, and the stink of burning flesh filled the air. The crematorium could not cope, so the S.S. caused funeral pires of logs to be built many metres square, and these were piled high with wood and corpses, so that a gigantic pall of smoke rose nearly a kilometre high above the camp, and the pestilential stench became worse. "Foul smells, misery and piles of corpses, that was what we had daily before our eyes". Dr. Leo says altogether 50,000 people died in this camp in the previous two-and-a-half months.

Conditions when the army took over

All figures are unreliable, but the camp appears to have contained some 60,000 people in the worst possible conditions of overcrowding, starvation, squalor and disease. The Army had been at work for 6 days before the Red Cross teams arrived. All the soldiers working in Camp 1 were volunteers. So moved were they by the frightful condition of the internees that they had given up their month's ration of sweets and cigarettes on their behalf, and a neighbouring unit also gave up their blankets.

The camp consisted of about a square mile of army huts, divided into three blocks, the Men's Lager, the Women's Lager, and outside the inner wire, the S.S. quarters. Conditions in the Camp were not too bad until January 1945, it seems, when there was vast influx of internees from camps further east. But when the British arrived, internees were packed at about 600 per large army hut, without running water or working sanitation. They had had nothing to eat for a week; before that for two months they had had 1 pint of swede soup each per day; before that for four months 2 pints of swede soup and a piece of bread each per day. They were dying at the rate of 600 per day of starvation and disease. Typhus was endemic.

The impression of the first to enter was of an enormous horde of people reduced to the animal level. Cannibalism was said to have been witnessed by a Major of the R.A.M.C. and is referred to in some detail in Dr. Fritz Leo's account. Among the heaps of dead the living wandered, excreting and treading in excretion. In some of the huts, the sights, smells and sounds were beyond endurance. Everywhere was the vast concourse of scarecrow people, bodies incredibly emaciated, and faces stamped with a single expression of despair.

The cleaning-up process

Fortunately for the internees and the Army, only a mile from the concentration camp were the barracks and buildings of a Wehrmacht Tank School, which made an ideal reception area for the internees from the camp. The Army's plan was to evacuate the camp entirely and then burn it. The central blocks of the Tank School were turned into a hospital, and the outlying ones as accommodation for 'fit' internees, who were housed in separate blocks according to nationality, while awaiting evacuation to a camp from which they were to be repatriated. As the evacuation would take some time, an effort was made to improve conditions in Camp 1 for the internees awaiting evacuation, by better food supplies, improving the water supply by chlorinating it, improving the drains, and setting up a First-Aid-Post cum Out-Patients Department.

Camp number 2, the Wehrmacht barracks and training camp, was described by one Team member as follows: "The houses were two-storey and were said to have been built since the beginning of the War; certainly they were not more than a few years' old. The Wehrmacht did not work in the Concentration Camp. This was a very large camp, which was put to good use to house the hospital of nearly 7,000 beds (later the number reached 11,000:ed.), and the majority of the British and internee workers. The camp's administrative offices were situated there too. The small houses, amidst silver birches and pines, were very attractive, there was a lake and a cinema, and modern slipper-baths. Indeed, comparisons were odious..."

Camp number 3 was an annexe of Camp number 2. It seems to have been used by the Germans as a barracks for the Hungarian guards who worked in and around No.1 Camp. The houses were similar to those in Camp No.2. It was now used as a transit camp for internees as the first stage of their journey home. Another camp, Camp 4 was rumoured to exist but this team member did not know where it was!

My own impressions and experiences are recorded as follows:-

When we arrived at Belsen we were quartered in the now empty Panzer Barracks about a mile north of the Camp. This consisted of more than a dozen large squares of barrack blocks, with a hospital wing and the officer's mess situated across a little dip in the ground and past a lake. A plan of these barracks survives, which we made as a guide to finding the different hospital blocks and quarters.

It was a Saturday night when we arrived and we were exhausted and glad to rest. On Sunday morning after a shower in the luxurious green marble showers provided for officers and situated near our quarters, we were cleaning the dirt from our vehicles and carrying out servicing tasks when the call came for us to proceed immediately to the Belsen Camp in order to evacuate the children. This was the first we had heard of the presence of any children there, and it may surprise the reader as it did us to learn that there were several hundred mostly orphan children in a separate hut situated in a distant part of the Camp. Upon our arrival at the Camp, which was only a short drive of a mile or so down the road from the barracks, we were directed to a hut in a separate part of the Camp where a number of motherly ladies were looking after what we understood to be children orphaned by the death of their parents or separated from them. Naturally they were given first priority in the evacuation. Letters record there were no less than 237 children in the block when we arrived (Dr. Fritz Leo's account speaks of 700 children in Camp 1). I had a chat with the motherly lady who had been looking after the children in this part of the camp. "She lay ill in bed in a dimly lit hut. Although very weak, she talked with authority (albeit through an interpreter). She offered me a chair but it was not safe to tarry long in any of these horrible huts, and I took my leave quickly and went on my way." All I can remember is the sickening feeling as I had to pass a truck on the way to this particular spot in the Camp and passed very near to if not actually with my wheel over the edge of a pile of stinking and partly decomposed bodies lying alongside the road and awaiting burial. These piles of bodies were everywhere, and little groups of inmates huddled over wood fires staring helplessly or picking over the bodies to see what useful clothing, etc. could be rescued.

The main part of the Camp consisted of a wide road lined by large wooden huts which contained literally hundreds of inmates, who lay on

Bodies in Belsen Camp were buried in communal graves

wooden bunks on two or three levels. In the morning a party of men carried out those who had died in the night and deposited them on one of the rotting piles of corpses some distance away across the road. There was what could be described as a primitive medical room, known as the Krankenhaus, to which some of our team were assigned to carry out first aid work and administer what medicines were available. Parties of Hungarian soldiers manned the main gate and served as orderlies in the Camp, while the few German troops who had remained on the site (members of the Wehrmacht not the Waffen SS who had fled) were employed in collecting the bodies and taking them to the large communal graves which were eventually organised and dug by the Army with bulldozers. Today these sites are marked with mounds in the Belsen Memorial Grounds, bearing the inscription "Here lie 5000 dead" and "Here lie 2000 dead". But it is quite impossible for the visitor today to evoke the atmosphere of those days. One has to pinch oneself to believe that it could have been so. This indeed I did several times when I visited with my wife in 1988 the beautifully-kept heather-covered memorial grounds into which the Camp has now been turned.

I did not see much of Camp 1 after my initial visit, although I did go there several times to assist in the evacuation of 'walking wounded'. Several days we waited around all day with our ambulances in the Camp, waiting in vain for work to be assigned to us. Once I went to help two of our men who were trying to trace the drainage system and unblock it with what I believe is known in German as a 'schlammpumpe' or pressure hose. I don't think they had much success. In the smoke from the little fires lit by the inmates one could see dimly a wasteland of filth and litter where the sun did not seem to shine. But the appearance of the Camp rapidly improved. One day I had evacuated 17 Hungarian and Polish women whom I described as a terrible group of sad and feeble women - many of them half dead (May 11). Already by May 1st I recorded that things had greatly improved in the last nine days. "I saw only one dead body by the roadside. Bulldozers have cleared the ground between the huts. There are latrines - wooden boxes in the open. There is a Medical Inspection (M.I.) room and a small hospital. Also a bath and cleaning station for able-bodied people, & registration was taking place by the Military Government of the inmates prior to evacuation". We spent some time ferrying patients to the Hospital within the camp and to the 'rivieres' or cleaned-up blocks which had by this time been established as temporary accommodation. Jane concentrated her efforts on work with the Jews who survived, spending part of the time in Camp 1, and her account of her impressions of the conditions in Camp 1 at this time is given in Appendix 8.

Apart from rescuing the children, perhaps my most vivid recollection of

Army flame throwers move in

the Camp was the day the burning ceremony took place. I went down there to attend with Ted B., the Red Cross worker who had become such a close friend of our Team because he shared our pacifist views and had taken to joining us frequently on social occasions. Setting fire to the huts was preceded by speeches from a General and the local military commanders, who then aimed the first blazes from the flame-throwers. Generous tributes were paid to all who had given such invaluable assistance towards clearing the Camp. When the signal was given the flame-throwers attacked one of the barrack blocks which had been adorned with a German flag and a large portrait of Hitler, to the sound of great cheering. Rebuilding the shattered lives of those whose health had been undermined or whose minds had been scorched by the experience of being inmates would take longer than those few minutes of symbolic and deeply satisfying destruction, and for some could never be complete.

The records in my possession give a tally of those who were placed in hospital wards in the Panzer Barracks in the weeks which had preceded the burning. Each day for several weeks we received about 600 patients to be hospitalized in the former Panzer Barracks. Army transport brought them from the Camp to the Disinfestation Centre inside the perimeter, where they were cleaned and scrubbed, initially by British Army nurses from a Casualty Clearing Unit, later replaced by a party of German nurses. Then a fleet of ambulances ferried the patients to the different hospital wings situated in the many squares of the Barracks. I was on this so-called 'clean run' most of the time, with my Austin four-bed ambulance usually carrying five patients at a time, one on the floor in the middle. In this situation, I became a frequent target of the growing number of press representatives, who were anxious to describe the situation and were on the look-out for stories. I also ferried the nurses to their accommodation for lunch and during these runs I had an opportunity to talk to some of them about the Camp and what had happened. 'Not all Germans are bad Germans', they insisted. 'We did not know these things were going on'.

By May 16th there were 11,259 in the hospital. At one point we had to suspend admissions because there were no more beds, and a party of vehicles set off to scour the countryside far and wide. On May 7th, 34 vehicles, including our two Bedfords one of which I drove, set off through Celle to Neustadt and Steinhude in search of beds. At the end of the day we had only found sufficient beds to fill two vehicles. The rest of us found our own way home only to discover great excitement and celebrations, Verey signal lights being fired green, red, blue, white and black - very impressive, and everyone was drinking like mad. The war in Europe was over and there were rumours that the King would broadcast to the nation on the morrow at 9 p.m.

In fact it was the next day May 8th 1945 that the hostilities ceased and this has since become known as VE Day. My memories of it concern a very long day's drive in the Bedford (we lost our way) with Joyce and the Padre to Osnabruck to fetch our NAAFI supplies. We reached Osnabruck at 3.30 p.m. after driving since 8 a.m. (a distance of only 155 miles). We collected a disappointing load of cigarettes and chocolate, etc. and set off on our return journey at 5.45 p.m. reaching our home base very tired at about midnight. We had seen many displaced persons on the move on the roads around Hannover. On the way back one rather drunken Russian soldier waved me to a stop and handed me a gun, which turned out to be a Verey pistol, a gun used for firing signal flares. Being a pacifist I handed it to the padre as a souvenir! Churchill had broadcast at 3 p.m. and the King at 9 p.m. but we missed it all. There were many parties and jollifications that night, my diary records.

While I was concerned with the 'clean run' to the hospital blocks, what were other members of the Team doing?

Team members' work

Kit B. was supervising the running of the canteen kitchens from which the hospital food was supplied, until illness prevented her from continuing. Jane spent two days on registration, was then transferred to the hospital, when the staff shortage became acute; and then to clothing distribution. She also interested herself in the plight of the many Jewish internees who had survived the holocaust, and spent many days talking to them and comforting them in Camp 1 before they could be evacuated. Some were soon transferred to other camps in Celle and Lingen, which Jane visited to report on the conditions and to help, and in the case of Lingen, she actually accompanied the party on the long and uncomfortable journey there, and was seconded to work in that camp before rejoining the Team later on. [Appendix 8 gives Jane's own account of her work in this respect]. Joyce also began by registering patients, and was later transferred to general hospital duties. Beth began in the Children's Home, supervised canteens for some days, was in charge of a whole nursing block for a while before taking over with Jane the issue of clothing to internee staff, and the growing number of convalescent patients. Lilian, being an S.R.N., was placed in charge of one of the squares of 5 hospital houses. Marjorie transported people and supplies of all sorts to and from the hospital. Bill R. and Bill B. had been purifying the water supply to Camp 1, chlorinating the water, and improving the condition of the drains (this was a job which they ferreted out for themselves). Michael, together with Red Cross workers from other teams, had been running a First Aid Post in Camp 1. Hugh was concerned with ferrying the Hungarians to and from Camp 1 in the three-tonner. He also developed an extremely useful role in collecting fresh vegetables from the surrounding country-side, unofficially at first but later on he received official permission. Lyn was engaged on a variety of work, originally concerned with getting supplies of all sorts for the internees; and later doing extremely useful jobs which appeared to be nobody else's business, e.g. coping with the problems of the bath-house which was used both by the Army and Red Cross personnel. She later became responsible for the messing and billeting arrangements of the whole Red Cross Commission.

Organisation of the Hospital

The army had been able to evacuate an average of 600 patients a day from Camp 1, beginning with the women and children, and afterwards the men. Patients were brought to the cleansing station, wrapped only in blankets. There they were washed thoroughly, heads shaved if necessary, and powdered with A.L.63. They were then taken to the receiving blocks, which had been prepared by the RAMC. The reception of the patients was in the hands of a

Q.A. nurse, who sometimes had internees to help her. Originally, the Q.A.'s stayed only for one day in each block, moving on to a new block the next day. On the next day, two BRCS workers took over, to help the internee staff get organised. On the third day, one BRCS worker was sent and usually no further BRCS workers could be spared for the fourth and subsequent days. In some houses the internee staff were quite capable of organising the place adequately; in others, it was complete chaos. With the arrival of further personnel (RAMC, Swiss Red Cross, English medical students and German doctors and nurses) four of the squares originally opened up were put under BRCS sisters, with other BRCS nurses to help. The A.W.Q.A. nurses managed different blocks.

Staffing and running of hospital blocks

The central blocks of the main barracks which were the first to be turned into a hospital consisted of a series of 11 open squares. Each had a canteen at one end and two large houses on either side. These houses consisted of two floors and a loft, containing about 32 rooms. Each floor had a washroom and WC's, with the only running water in the building. There was no means of cooking or heating water except on top of the ordinary heating stoves in each room. Wards contained from 3 to 12 beds, and the average capacity of each house was 150 beds, with about 70 beds in 2 large wards in the canteen blocks. All food was cooked in canteen kitchens, and carried by Hungarian soldiers to the different blocks in the square in various containers, usually open buckets. Internee staff ate in the canteens. One night some Hungarian soldiers were caught taking a bath in one of the large urns in which the soup was prepared in the kitchens!

The internee staff in each house usually consisted of a doctor (at first shared between two houses), a trained nurse, and anything up to 12 other women and girls who might possibly have had some previous nursing experience; 80% of these were convalescent typhus cases who should not have been working at all, let alone 12 hours a day. There were also four Hungarian soldiers under an English orderly, who did the heavy cleaning, stretcher-bearing, etc. Eventually a group of German doctors and nurses was imported to help, and these were scattered throughout the various blocks. The reception which the Germans received varied greatly, and was largely conditioned by the personality and general attitude of the individual German concerned. In one house at least, the nurse was received with very little hostility by the Polish and Russian staff and the Jewish patients. She assured us that most people in Germany had no conception of what was going on in these camps, and said that she was thankful to have the chance of working for the victims. Similar affirmations were made by many others. Some even asserted implausibly that Hitler himself did not know.

Little real nursing was done at all. Attention was concentrated on trying to keep the patients clean, warm and fed - no easy matter when diarrhoea was prevalent and hot water almost unobtainable. On two successive days, the main water supply broke down altogether and was cut off for over 9 hours. Such refinements as temperature charts had been achieved in one or two houses at most; but a fair supply of drugs was eventually obtained and all patients received vitamin tablets.

The general condition of the patients admitted to the hospital was shocking - emaciated to a degree, and prematurely aged, suffering from famine oedema and other conditions arising from avitaminosis and starvation as well as typhus. Food was a major problem. Convalescents complained bitterly that they did not get enough and watch had to be kept to see that national animosities did not result in preferential treatment for some patients and neglect of others. Supplies were short at times but hunger was no safe indication of what the patient's weakened digestion could stand, and there were many relapses through overeating. Further complications arose as relations came visiting, bringing food from outside, and from convalescents wandering round, wrapped in blankets, picking up food scraps from the dustbins, which they cooked over little wood fires among the shrubs and bushes.

General problems

At the very beginning an effort was made to register all patients, but shortage of staff forced the relief workers to abandon this until further help arrived. The result was that great difficulty was experienced in re-uniting families separated by the evacuation. Pathetic groups of people wandered from one ward to another, looking for their relatives. Many people were brought in unconscious, and died before their names could be taken. Fortunately eventually registration was resumed, but this work suffered from being understaffed and sometimes lists were incomplete.

Convalescent patients were only too willing to talk, and tell how their families had been gassed, buried alive or burned, in other camps. The main preoccupation of all was how to contact their families and friends who might still be alive somewhere. A limited number of D.P. field postcards were available, but these gave no address so that relatives could not reply.

French, Belgian, Dutch and Czech citizens were anxious to return home. Hungarians and Russians were very uncertain about their future; while of course the big problem was that of the Poles. The non-Jewish Poles feared to return to a Poland dominated by Russia; and the Jews had no desire to return and asked piteously where they *could* go. Some internees began escaping from the camps and trekking home along the roads and terrorising the local population in their search for food and clothes, and even stateless people were unwilling to stay in camps indefinitely.

Jane vividly describes the "lager" mentality of the internees, how their cheerfulness at first turned to some sourness later, as their conditions improved, and they began to have the strength to complain about almost everything! Above all else they were concerned to locate their families and friends from whom they had often been separated in the camps. Many were in despair about the future, being destitute and homeless. In a description of "life in the Camp now" Jane describes the improved conditions in Camp 1 by the 6th May 1945, and her experiences in talking to inmates about the conditions they had endured there and in other camps in Poland, how they were marched here in the depth of winter, etc. A particularly eloquent passage describes the work of the internee doctors and the care they took in their examination of each person.

Jane also recounts how she was with an Austrian and a Yugoslav Jewish doctor on the evening of 4th May, when a Polish nurse burst into the room, sobbing bitterly, that the War had ended, and she had no home, no family, no friends, where should she go?

The Clothing Store

The Clothing Store was promptly nick-named Harrods by the troops, and Ted B. was concerned with this work. I helped him for a while with this, in between my ambulance duties. The demand for our services to ferry patients to hospital was by this time dropping off, and consideration was being given to assigning us to other duties. I was to begin a welfare job in Camp 2, and had attended a conference of welfare officers to meet the Camp Welfare Officer, Lieut. H. We had a most useful discussion on various aspects of the work, particularly the absence of information on which to base any welfare advice and policies, and the need to know more about official policy. I introduced myself to the Major in charge at 618 Mil.Gov., Major L. and the Rumanian interpreter Gross, who spoke seven languages. Gross was an engineer who had studied in Paris and had worked for Cadbury's in Birmingham. I toured the Camp with him and found that conditions varied between the different ethnic groups : the Poles were living in good conditions but the Yugoslavs and Italians were in a bad situation. I made a point of

Ambulance work at Belsen, en route to the clothing store

going back later to see a Yugoslav diplomat called Bogdan and the Secretary of the Polish Committee. The former took me to see the Yugoslav liaison officer and the latter took me to see the Polish liaison officer. All this was in preparation for assuming my new role as a welfare officer.

I have been asked many times about my reaction to the appalling conditions and circumstances we encountered at Belsen. All I can say is that at the time we could not afford to have any emotional feelings about the situation, we simply got on with the daily tasks in hand and postponed any personal feelings we may have had. This is confirmed in my discussion with several surviving Team members. There may have been adverse reactions which occurred later, however. But you could not possibly do this work if you kept on having feelings about what was going on and what lay behind it all. I have reflected many times since that nothing that I did as a conscientious objector speeded the release of those poor people from their suffering or brought about the collapse of the 'evil empire' which was Nazi Germany. I did feel at the time a sense of guilt and shame about this, and since then I have mentioned it to several people who were interested enough to inquire. Many years later one woman psychologist from Berlin, to whom I had related my story, described me as deeply insecure, but I have never been conscious of this fact, if indeed it is true.

A fresh test of my pacifist convictions was provided by the Falklands War and the Gulf War. My response is usually along these lines, and it is a personal response, and should not be attributed to any other members of the Team. I was glad that I had the opportunity to do what I did in the way of humanitarian service. I do not think I would even now be able to join an organisation that might require me to drop bombs on innocent people. I have never believed that the end justifies the means. I hope that in my life I have borne witness to my profound belief that the preservation of human life and humane values should prevail over all other considerations, however pressing and convincing. At the same time, I am prepared to concede that this may be a wrong approach, and the contradiction between my pacifist beliefs deeply held and the reality of the evils we have to confront in our daily lives makes me sad and provokes guilty feelings. I am conscious of the contradictions entailed in our having worked so closely with the military, while being pacifist in our convictions. I did what I thought was right at the time, and am glad to have been privileged to be given the chance to alleviate a little of the world's suffering when the opportunity arose. I found it rather amusing to be placed in charge of a troop train carrying military personnel on leave, or to fly home from Germany on my discharge in an RAF transport. Incidentally, that posed problems when we landed at Farnborough since I had to go through customs as a civilian and there was no customs and immigration officer on hand to deal with me, so they had to send for one!

CHAPTER 4

The Interim Period at Sulingen-Bei-Diepholz

THE VERY NEXT DAY after I had been discussing the new 'welfare' role which I was to undertake, we were told we were about to leave Belsen, and that I had to wind up the work within a few days. I was very sorry about this, as we were just about to start work on our new assignments. I had the painful task of telling Major L. of our impending departure and tying up the loose ends. We set about packing the three-tonner and the other vehicles. We moved off on May 25th at noon. Lyn and Bill R. had gone ahead in an advance party. We crossed the rivers Aller and Weser via Fallingbostel and Reddin and arrived at Sulingen, after a 65 mile journey. This was where we had stayed overnight on the way up to Belsen. We were attached to 822 Mil.Gov. Needless to say they were not expecting us, nor had they asked for us to come! They had requested a sanitary team!! Billets were arranged for us in a private house, Mike and I sharing a room with the first beds since we left Middlekerke. We were to work in a Refugee Transit Camp, which served as a collecting point for the thousands of displaced persons in the area, and from which transports were arranged to their home countries. Thousands passed through the rail-head there en route for Belgium, Holland and France every day. I was asked to assist in the business of registration, under Capt Q. of 822 Mil.Gov. He took me to the railway station, where I saw a train of fifty coaches each holding thirty people leave at 11 a.m. on May 26th. I thought the way they had organised themselves into groups, were issued with hard rations, and were decorating each carriage with tree branches most interesting.

They were only allowed to take one bag, suitcase or pack with them, so had to jettison the rest at the assembly point. Some of our Team members were put to work salvaging what could be useful from the pile of discarded baggage. Once again, the grey uniforms led to some misunderstanding, they

Repatriation westward from Sulingen, May 1945

were mistaken for Germans, and some of the items were thrown at them as they were discarded by the displaced persons.

Later I went to the Milkerei, which housed one thousand persons, and saw the arrangements for supervising their arrival and billeting. A loudspeaker directed the Army transports as they arrived in the large parade ground or assembly area. I was allocated the services of an extremely attractive Dutch girl to act as my interpreter, and actually on several occasions directed the Army trucks as they drove in how to line up and disembark their passengers. This was the first time I had heard my voice on a loudspeaker system, quite an experience! I assumed the language of command, I remember, without much difficulty, though it was a curious role for a conscientious objector to find himself directing British Army drivers. (I have more details about these transports.)

The two Bills busied themselves with the sanitation system. We all helped with the salvage work, (no less than 150 blankets were salvaged) and with cleaning out fresh barns and sheds on the farms to serve as additional accommodation, for the numbers were increasing daily. German women helped to clean out the sheds and demonstrated, not for the first time, their capacity for hard work and quick results! Hugh busied himself visiting the French hospital, where he found some Spanish patients, and helped collect supplies from the surrounding farms and villages for distribution there. One should note in passing that his wife Juanita, who came from Spain, initially had not been free to join us as a member of the Team, which she joined much later at Brunswick.

One day we took two ambulances and a Bedford truck with 32 patients to Rheine, where there was a large camp for French D.P.s, mostly POWs. Half our party went on the Lingen to visit another Team member, Jane, who had left us at Belsen to go and work with this camp of Jewish survivors of the holocaust. The other half (including me) returned to base, a round trip of 187 miles, four hours each way. At Rheine we came across the United Nations Relief and Refugee organisation known as UNRRA for the first time. They had 10-15 vehicles. Passing through German towns like Osnabruck I noted once more the severe war damage, with rubbish piled high on the pavements each side of the main streets, and several areas completely derelict.

A few days later I went with Beth to Lingen via Rheine to take Miss R., dropping off two patients and four sitting cases at Rheine as we passed through. After having supper with Jane we returned on non-military roads using German road signs and directions from some civilians and cut an hour off the journey and saved many miles. Outward the journey had been via Minden and the roundabout military routes signposted at the time (155 miles). The return journey was only 76 miles! But it was an adventurous thing to do at that time in post-war Germany.

By June 4 we had heard we were on the move again. Kiel or Lubeck were mentioned as possible destinations. We were invited to supper at the Officers Mess before our departure, and we had a great discussion as to whether we could possibly drink toasts to the King, to the Armed Forces, etc. In the event the dinner was quite informal and not so boring as we had expected. In fact the officer in charge of 822 Mil Gov., Major W., was very anxious to please and be friendly. He had actually asked for us to accompany him.

By June 8th it had been decided we were to go to Braunschweig (Brunswick in the English language). Lyn and the Major went off on a *recce* (reconnaissance visit). On their return late at night they told us the situation they had found. There were about 47,000 D.P.s in the town, and more in the surrounding districts. They consisted of Poles and Russians mainly, with an admixture of different nationalities in small numbers. The Major was to be in command of the refugee camps in the whole area.

CHAPTER 5

The work with Displaced Persons in the Brunswick Area

WE LEFT SULINGEN at 9.00 a.m. on Sunday morning June 10th 1045, after an early breakfast. There was a kind farewell from our German hosts, who seemed to think well of us. We passed through Nienburg and Neustadt and on to the autobahn, heading east. The road had been heavily bombed all the way, and we could see many craters on the adjoining land. A sign read '200 kilometres to Berlin'. We were impressed by the provision of lay-bys at intervals on the motorway, complete with concrete picnic tables and seating, which we had never seen before. After skirting Hannover and stopping for a picnic lunch, we found we were only 170 kilometres from the Berlin Ring road, i.e. 125 miles. We took the exit to Braunschweig (Brunswick) and as soon as we reached the outskirts of the town we turned off into Siegfriedstrasse, a street of flats and houses, where we came to a halt. Major W. was there to welcome us and we found to our surprise the choice of six flats awaited us, and German labour available to assist, albeit rather unwillingly, with unloading the vehicles. Two little girls came into our flat, very moved by our occupation of the flat which they had vacated only the day before. They asked if they could look for some of their toys. We made it clear that we should respect their property.

Bill R. and I shared a flat consisting of two bedrooms, sitting room, kitchenette, bathroom and lavatory. The local inhabitants seemed curious and rather surly, more spirited in their resistance to the occupation of their flats than we had experienced before at Sulingen.

We took time to visit the centre of the city and familiarise ourselves with our new surroundings. The city had been very badly damaged by bombing, especially within the central area which was surrounded by a canal, river and moat system. We understood that most of the damage had occurred in one raid. This was the saturation bombing we had heard about! My description in a letter reads: "Inside the ring of old water defences lies a mass of rubble through which the cleared roads wind their way. Derelict churches vie with solitary chimney stacks to point the way through the chaos, and all is very dead and soul-less. I hear that most of the damage was in a 23-minute raid".

The owner of the flat which I shared with Bill R. was a miller's engineer, who had taken an interest in a Gliding Club since 1929, which was then almost a para-military organisation. His two charming daughters, aged 14 and 12, were keen members of the Hitler Youth, and his wife belonged to the Deutsche Frauenbund. So much we gleaned from the records they left behind in their flat. We also found some Nazi literature and Nazi school textbooks, which I thought were quite perverse. There was a most interesting political atlas, and the Rules of the Nazi Party. A list of the principles started with the affirmation that Adolf Hitler is always right, and continued with pious statements about duty, honour and service, ending with this gem: "Right is what serves Germany".

In the first week we completed a survey of the area allotted to us. This included the Hindenburg barracks and the Siegfried Kaserne. The former consisted of massive barrack blocks, which we deemed suitable for our purpose of housing displaced persons. An American officer and a master sergeant showed us around, and treated us to a massive lunch, ending up with coffee and doughnuts! We also inspected a Russian-Polish camp at Lehre which was reputed to be experiencing an epidemic of bed bugs. We found several and thought there could be no doubt about it. The Russian displaced persons there, however, seemed very clean and were pleasantly disposed towards us.

At the end of the first week I was able to re-visit Belsen with Bill B. There I found a letter from Rudolf Kustermeier, and later visited him and we had lunch together. I now discovered that he was living with a Latvian woman whom he had met in the camps. [Appendix 2 deals with my encounters with this German ex-concentration camp inmate.]

The following week, while some Team members stayed to supervise the cleaning-up by German labour of the Siegfried Kaserne, other members of the Team continued the search for accommodation. I spent a day with Lilian touring the neighbourhood prospecting for other camps and visiting existing D.P. camps. We also assisted with our transport some Polish and Belgian girls who were setting out to return to France and the west. The prospecting and visiting of camps continued into a third week. Other members of the

Team were busy surveying other camps in the area. The situation in the town was pretty chaotic, there being still present some units of the American forces and some Russian troops as well as the British Army, all of whom had to be accommodated somewhere. In addition, there were thousands of displaced persons of various nationalities milling around in search of a better place and food and clothing. The harassed British Town Major whose responsibility it was to sort out the billets expressed the view that the RAF should be made to do it: "after all, they bombed the place in the first instance!", which seemed a not inappropriate comment on this crazy situation.

One of the Team, looking out of the window of the flats we occupied in Siegfriedstrasse, noticed a group of American soldiers started a game of football with some young German boys, while their mothers looked on somewhat disapprovingly. It was rather too soon perhaps to try to make friends with the children of our former enemies, so recently defeated in battle and bombed to smithereens.

The Camp at Lehre

I wrote a report for Major W. about the accommodation available. As a result I was asked to act as Reception Officer for one of the camps which Major B. was filling up with Poles on exchange with the Russians. With one of the other officers I visited the camp at Lehre, which was some miles north-east of Braunschweig. There I met Thomas, the Polish camp commandant, and arranged for the Russian camp to be guarded when the Russians left. I also met the Russian camp leaders, and exchanged pleasantries with them (which as I recall involved my first encounter with vodka, which I was called upon to drink a tumbler-full neat and in one gulp and with difficulty refused a refill!). I warned them not to destroy the huts as they left, as others would be coming into the accommodation immediately. I also saw the local burgermeister and left orders for labour to be available the next day and sent a note to the local R.A. to be sure to provide protection for the camp. Later the same day I visited another camp, the Voigtlander Camp, where 1,000 displaced persons had already arrived, and half of them were sleeping on straw rather than use the bug-infested beds. I took some patients to the hospital.

The next morning Joyce and I left early for the camp at Lehre, where I took over from the Russians, 550 of whom were about to depart. Some had decamped in the night rather than be repatriated. There was a body in the water-tank, which was never identified. The buildings were thankfully still sound but the conditions inside them were pretty appalling, with litter and

Polish wedding in the displaced persons' camp at Lehre

filth everywhere, and we were faced with the need to clean them up speedily in order to be ready to receive the Polish displaced persons who were coming in exchange that evening, by the same transports which had taken the Russians. We were without any labour force at first, and in the afternoon one of the Polish liaison officers made a stirring appeal to the Poles already there to provide help, which brought an immediate and gratifying response of sixty volunteers. We also required the burgermeister to provide some assistance from local farms. The camp was cleared of muck and debris by eight in the evening. We received delivery of mountains of straw from the local farms, and some farm labourers and their women-folk came to help with the cleaning. We needed a radio van to control the reception, and I was provided with a small Opel fitted with two loudspeakers which I drove for a week or more, and here my experience at Sulingen proved useful. The reception went well, an excellent meal was provided for the 600 new arrivals, and we finished work at midnight. The next morning 250 more Poles arrived, with a prospect of a further 500. We agreed to accept the 250 but not the 500, and they were allocated accommodation. Many problems had to be sorted out at short notice. An ambulance case had to be taken to hospital, covers had to be ordered for the tops of the latrines. A French medical mission came and powdered 450 persons. We visited the local munitions factory where we found some useful materials and equipment, such as mine parts which could be used as excellent building blocks in the nursery school.

It was with some relief that on Sunday several of us went for a drive in the Opel with the Polish liaison officer, a crazy driver, to the neighbouring Harz mountains, via Bad Harzburg and Goslar.

The work at Lehre continued into a second week. A long list of requisites was delivered to the local Royal Artillery unit. The R.A. Captain was very helpful, providing some wood and the loan of their sanitation man. With his assistance we opened up the surface water drain, cleaned two sets of latrines, each with fourteen "holes", pumped the cess-pits clear, and opened up two new deep-trench latrines for which tops were provided. We raided the munitions factory once again for useful items. The situation in the town from the point of view of the administration was extremely chaotic, the military being responsible for the local government agencies, but they were not really in control and in the confusion we were often blamed for the failings of others. The Americans had pulled out by this time, leaving very little sign of organisation. They had certainly failed to tackle the displaced persons problem. But they had started a good local newspaper.

My week was interrupted when I spent a day taking the French Red Cross to the nearby city of Hildesheim to collect some Frenchmen; there was one bed-patient and four sitting patients. The town, which was a very old and picturesque city, had been 'pretty thoroughly erased', according to my diary.

There followed more visits to Lehre to receive more demands for help, and deal with many problems. Labour was in short supply, and various essentials were unavailable. There were many complaints emanating from the local commandant. A demarche was necessary, and I visited the RA's and the local burgermeister to seek assistance. By this time we were planning to open a school the following week, desks had already been provided and there was lino on the floor!

I made another day visit to Belsen, but this time I failed to find Kustermeier. Some said he had had a relapse and was in hospital, others that he had gone to Hannover to visit, others said he went to Sulingen with the British Red Cross representative Miss B., so I returned disappointed.

The school at Lehre had started and by now there were three classes as well as the kindergarten. The school ran in two sessions, one for the toddlers running from 9 till 11.00, then the older children from 11 till 1.00 p.m.

There was also a nursery school. They used paper from the munitions factory to write on, with pencils from the drawing office. They played with pieces of wood used in making mines and some round bobbins. Frocks were made from the material which was used for lining shells filled with cordite. Brushes had been found which were convex in shape because they were used for cleaning the inside of gun barrels, but the glass bowls we were delighted to discover which we thought of using as desert bowls provided unsuitable as they were so fragile, being parts used in the manufacture of mines, which shattered very easily.

I remained at Lehre for the next few weeks, during which time I went on a search for window glass to a glass factory at Gifhorn, which used to make perfume bottles, but they had none. Thence on further to Fallersleben to the site of the People's Car Factory (the Volkswagen), where in the middle of the vast works and labour camps I found a Friends Ambulance Unit team, with some team members with whom I was acquainted. They were running the D.P. camps and were expecting to handle Russians going east in transit in the very near future. This was July 7th, and my diary ceases at this point, apart from one brief entry in August, so that I have to rely on other sources for my recollections.

Fortunately I wrote home regularly to my parents in Wales giving detailed accounts of what I had been doing the previous week, and they preserved all or most of these letters together with some daily and weekly reports and miscellaneous papers, in a file from which I can reconstruct the following story.

CHAPTER 6

"Gypsy Camp", Brunswick and the work of Repatriation

AT ABOUT THIS time we were called upon to administer a large displaced persons camp to the west of Brunswick city, situated on an airfield in Broitzemerstrasse, which was known as "Gypsy Camp", a name given it by its previous occupants, the American forces. The Poles who came to live there named it after one of their national heroes, Tadeusz Kosciusko. Later it was labelled Quaker Centrum. Officially it was known as Assembly Centre 296 or Polish Camp 119. It consisted of the airfield with grass runways and a large administration building, several empty garages which could be used as warehouses, and a line of barrack blocks in squares which constituted living accommodation of a reasonable barracks type. There were two central cookhouses or large kitchens, and various other buildings which in time we eventually turned into a school and a church, a hospital wing and clinic. There was also a railway line connecting to the main railway network to the west of Braunschweig.

Opposite the Camp was a line of semidetached houses which were presumably occupied by the officers and their families, and it was here that we were billeted, occupying a house on the right side, looking from the gate, while the Military Government officers and other ranks occupied the houses to the left side. There was ample room to park our vehicles outside, and a good view of the main gate, with its guardhouse, where a Polish military police force manned the gate, checking comings and goings, for one had to have a pass to leave the Camp or be given permission as to enter as a visitor. We also organised a Camp police force, which dealt with internal order, and provided its own problems at times by its overbearing behaviour.

"Gypsy Camp", Brunswick. The main entrance and Guard Room

Our task was to receive thousands of Polish people, men women and children, who were being assembled here prior to repatriation. They were collected from their billets in camps and houses and farms in the area, where they had been what we would now call guest workers, or what were really forced labour. They were moved by the Army in trucks, and we had to register them and powder them on arrival, issuing an Identity Card which entitled them to food, and generally see to their welfare. Little did we imagine at first the problems we were to encounter in this humanitarian exercise. One would think it would be all sweetness and light, but before we finished the task we had encountered strikes and exploitation, illicit stills and even one homicide.

One letter recounts a visit with Joyce and Lilian to the Rathaus, the town-hall, which was situated right in the heart of the old town. This must have been a very beautiful old town, enclosed by the river and canals, and with quaint narrow streets and good shops. My sighting of a tram caused some excitement : it was the first I had seen in the Centre, though trams had been running in the outlying suburbs. There were occasional trains too.

At the Rathaus, Joyce was trying to secure some baby clothes at the Polish Committee, while Lilian was raising a fuss about milk for the children. The supply problems were, I remarked, difficult to describe. We were almost helpless because, with all the goodwill in the world, if you lack essentials like potatoes, soap, cobblers' tools, palliasse covers, baby's teats, sewing materials, needles and thread, thimbles, paper, pencils, beds, coal, etc. - the list of things difficult to get really covered everything you could think of - the good you could do was negligible. We were all very depressed and worried about the situation, and I wrote home begging them to send items ostensibly for my personal use, since officially it was not allowed to send things freely, and I requested especially occupational materials, needles and thread, wools, and old Christmas cards for the nursery school. Almost every letter home contains a request for such items as these, and even a date-stamp (for the registration office) and a glass-cutter! A ready response was forthcoming from a variety of sources, and I was very pleased to receive some food parcels from my aunt in Canada, and a fruit cake which we eagerly consumed!

I doubted it was simply a matter of organisation, and considered that the supply problems formed only part of a larger problem. Even if the organisation were better, I doubted that the supplies could be found. Germany was being bled to the last ounce. The Displaced Person ration scale was fixed so as to provide a diet of 2000 calories a day, but that might not be sustained. German civilians got a ration calculated to give them 1800 calories a day, it was said. But by the winter it would have to be cut to 1300 calories a day, according to one UNRRA official. The prospect for Germany in the coming winter was indeed grave. The Quaker team was very concerned about the whole situation, and wished we could feel more effective in our miserable efforts to break through the nonchalant ineptitude of the administration so as to be able to render real service.

By this time we were delighted to learn of the arrival in the area of a second FRS Team and a team from the IVSP (International Voluntary Service for Peace). The former were situated at the neighbouring town of Goslar. There was also an FAU Team and a Save-The-Children team in the vicinity. Also UNRRA had teams working in the area, some of whose members I had met previously. We got together for Sunday afternoon tea and a service in the evening.

In mid-July I was asked to drive the three-ton Austin six-wheeler truck to the Rhineland to fetch gas for use in disinfesting buildings. I was accompanied by a German gas expert. We left early, at 7 a.m. and had various adventures en route. We took some food and expected to have to stay

The Blockleaders' Conference

The Cobblers' Workshop

"GYPSY CAMP"

The School. Lunchtime

Welfare interview

overnight. First we drove along the autobahn past Hannover, crossing the River Weser south of Minden near Bad Oeynhausen. The fan-belt on the lorry gave trouble, and I procured a new one and fitted it myself on the road, only to discover that it was too small. I drove to a REME workshops who fitted the right size, and we resumed our journey, driving like hell till we reached Dortmund, passing Herford, the headquarters of 21 Army Group, Bielefeld and Hamm. (Remember the nightly bombing of the marshalling yards there?) We left the autobahn at Dortmund since it was unusable because of bomb damage, and wandered through forests of broken telegraph posts, power lines, tram lines, factory chimneys, coal mines and steelworks, till we reached Hagen, crossing the River Ruhr and on to Wuppertal, turning there off the Dusseldorff road through Burscheid and Opladen. We reached Opladen at 9.45 p.m. and I discovered a puncture in one of the rear wheels. We decided to seek accommodation for the night, and drove on for five more miles before finding an inn where we were given a meal with Rhineland cider and were glad to reach bed at midnight. Up at 6 a.m. I tried to change the wheel, without success, so we went to a German garage and thence to a vulcanising works to have the tyre repaired. Thence to the Bayer factory at Leverkusen near Cologne, where we arranged to purchase the disinfestation gas. Dr. P., the sales manager and the other directors were very helpful, and asked many questions about agricultural chemistry and horticulture. They wanted to know whether the Colorado beetle was found in England : it was currently causing considerable damage in Germany. International agricultural chemistry journals lined the walls of the office, many in the English language and in French.

We left Leverkusen at 1.00 p.m. and after lunch in the hotel, we left Opladen at 2 p.m. and drove to the autobahn via Hagen, Iserlohn and Neheim, reaching it at 5.30 p.m. But it was not till 11 p.m. that we reached Brunswick, and by this time we were both very tired! I had driven 550 miles, partly over roads severely damaged by the war, and with a heavy load on my return journey, and I had never driven a three-tonner before!

(I have recorded this journey in some detail since it gives a picture of the difficulties of travel in post-liberation Germany at this time. Hugh had an almost identical experience at the end of June.)

The sequel to this episode was the discovery that the Siegfried Kaserne, which was supposed to have been disinfested with the gas and sealed off for a few days, had not in fact been so treated. One of our Team members, Bill R. happened to wander round the back of one of the barrack blocks and discovered a door swinging open. Upon investigation he could find no trace of gas inside the building, and inspection of all the other buildings proved negative also.

Needless to say, we dispensed with the services of the gas expert from that day.

My letters home comment on the new hatred which had grown up since the liberation. We were experiencing the beginnings of deep anti-German feelings and a new nastiness was in the air. This found expression in a variety of ways, and was particularly strong among the Poles, the Russians the French, the Belgians, and the Dutch, all of whom had suffered so gravely during the German occupation. The consequences of the widely held belief that all Germans were evil was the justification it gave to theft from farmers as well as in the towns, the killing of pigs, chickens, and even the odd cow or calf. Also the belief that only the Germans should be expected to do the heavy work in the new world, as slaves to those who themselves had so recently been enslaved. Adding to those feelings was the despair or lack of hope felt by many about returning to their own countries. Even some of the French had doubts about repatriation, it seems.

These feelings also found expression in the widely held belief that war against Russia was inevitable, indeed some even asked not when it would begin but how it was going? Some expressed the view that only a united Europe would be able to solve these problems. Some of my closest acquaintances among the D.P.s whom I had known in the concentration camp and in Brunswick believed that "here is one of the cardinal points of all work in the near future" in terms of education and politics. The Russians released from the camps had not been a very good advertisement, so many of them had gone wild on their release and turned to stealing, rape and murder. H.N. Brailsford had written in the New Statesman on June 16th 1945 something with which I strongly agreed: "The Nazis have indeed been crushed, but they have left behind them as an accursed legacy their racial theory in a new form, and with it, for our invitation, their models of ruthlessness".

My family collected and sent bits of material and clothing for distribution to the Poles and Ukrainians now in Lehre (there were 1020 at the end of July 1945). The silks went to the school for embroidery. At this time it seems that 10,000 sheets had been sent to Potsdam (in preparation for the Conference of the Great Powers) while we had a hospital without a single sheet! We had some success at this time in getting a supply of cigarettes and soap for the Camp at Lehre, but one packet of soap flakes had to be divided among eight persons.

At Gypsy Camp, Hugh had been busy preparing the buildings for the receipt of 3-4000 Poles. Lilian and I were assisting him. I was called in to arrange the Reception of the first 580 to arrive. Also I helped to organise work parties and sanitary squads to clean and prepare buildings. It was now 30th July and the first I heard about this assignment was that very morning! By now were were settled in the modern flat just outside the gates of the Gypsy Camp and about a mile from the centre of town. I shared a room with Michael. The place had been thoroughly looted before we arrived, and the German girl who cleaned up the mess was nearly in tears as she swept up the familiar rubble of spilled drawers and smashed cupboards. The room contained a sideboard with space for books, etc., a white wardrobe into which I unpacked all my belongings for the first time since we left London, one chair fit to sit on, a rather dirty-looking pouffe, and one broken chair. Also my camp bed, which served as a make-shift sofa.

I remained in this Camp the rest of my time in Germany, nearly a year, and witnessed and experienced many events and strange happenings. The early period was entirely occupied by receiving new batches of displaced persons and settling them in. Each day we received lorry-loads, everyone travelling in three-tonners open to the weather, with all their belongings on board. We sorted out their luggage first, depositing non-edible items in rooms set aside for disinfestation. A German team carried out this function. Tickets were issued for the baggage as in any cloakroom system. Then the newcomers had to submit to being powdered with AL63 (anti-lice powder which was really a form of DDT in powder guns, which we used quite freely, often having a joke by powdering each other unawares!). They then passed along a channel formed by tables to be registered by my staff. We took their names on DP2 Cards and issued them with a DP1 (Identity) card and a Food Card. The Food Card contained numbers up to 100 and two numbers were punched daily for meals.

My real headaches were (1) to stop others from different Camps not on the official removal list from taking up residence; (2) to keep out strays; (3) to ensure that the disinfestation was something like fifty-per cent effective; (4) to collect the Foodcards issued by the Burgermeister in Brunswick to these people; (5) to know exactly how many people were in the Camp, for feeding purposes; (6) to sort out the DP2 Cards according to the lists of residents supplied to us in due course by each Blockleader; (7) to prepare for and carry out a more thorough Registration at a later date.

On top of all this I seemed to have become a kind of general information bureau. Indeed all members of the Team were constantly engaged in counselling and giving advice and practical help.

Michael's task was to try and furnish the rooms ready for people to occupy when the arrived. We took all the air-raid beds in Brunswick, but there was never enough furniture. Often people arrived before there was a bed or room for them. Lilian tried to set up a sick-bay, and gathered all the furniture together in preparation for the opening, but as it was left unguarded in the night, it all vanished and she had to start again. She had a Polish nursing sister, one reliable cleaner and helper, two male medical orderlies who did nothing but grumble, and tried three or four different arrangements for doctors, each of which seemed to break down for some reason.

In August I was able to help the Polish priest to set up a chapel. A make-shift altar was provided in no time but there was no seating of any kind. In due course the altar was beautifully decorated using the tops of cans, some blue material, and bits of greenery. I attended some services there.

We had difficulty getting the Poles to work; because of the food shortage they were reluctant to expend energy. We were prohibited from giving food to the Germans who did work for us, and there was an energetic and loyal maintenance team under a foreman Willi who was a real find. I wrote at this time that the Germans hated us, the Poles disliked us, and by now we were by no means sure that we liked ourselves. Conditions were poor, and we foresaw trouble in the near future unless things improved and there was news about repatriation to Poland. As from August 15th there was a severe cut in the rations. Relations with the Army were not good.

I mention in one letter a week of comedy and tragedy. Suddenly we were stricken by some bug and nearly all members of the Team were affected, as well as the Military Government staff. The population of Brunswick was likewise affected, and I commented that it was just as well one didn't have to spend a penny each time one went to the loo!

The tragedy occurred when one day the Army arrived in force in the shape of the Military Police who were looking for Poles (from a village which had accepted none) in connection with the murder of a German. They arrived in half-a-dozen jeeps accompanied by some large armoured cars. They rounded up all the men in the Camp and took their watches. They then went round the rooms and took wireless sets and accordions. The result was a very ugly scene. Our commandant Hugh J. was summoned along with Jan the Polish liaison officer. There was little they could do to allay the wild resentment of the crowd which had gathered. In the end the Military Police were persuaded to give up the wirelesses, etc. (but they did not return the watches) and they left, saying that if anyone threw stones as they did so they would fire. This incident caused a good deal of ill-feeling and serious complaints were made to a higher level. My letter records that there was a notice in the Camp which read: 'Individual rights will be respected".

Early in August we heard the results of the General Election in the U.K. and there was much celebration. A Labour Government had been elected! It was hard to believe but the confirmation came through at six in the evening, and almost all the Team were delighted. The two Polish liaison officers who worked with us joined us for celebrations. Joyce had slices of her brother's wedding cake which she kindly shared with us. We had great fun speculating on who would hold which office in the Cabinet. I did not think the result of the election was greatly influenced by the Service vote since so many had been unable to vote or had failed to vote. I had come across some FAU who did not receive their papers. Some who did receive election voting papers tore them up, not wishing to cast their vote.

At this time we were still eating at the Mess in Siegfriedstrasse, situated in a tavern on the corner of the main road. It was a great nuisance to have to go there for every meal, and in due course separate arrangements were made for us to eat at our quarters outside the "Gypsy Camp", but this was not until early in November (November 5th).

In the middle of August 1945 we had an unforgettable week. A hunger strike started in one of the large Polish displaced persons camps, the Heinrich der Loewe Kaserne, where only a few weeks before I had been advising UNRRA officials about the arrangements. Barricades were placed across the gates so that no vehicles could enter. All military and UNRRA staff were obliged to leave their cars outside. To begin with they were not even allowed in on foot, but that did not last long. The following day by nine in the morning black flags had been hoisted at "Gypsy Camp" all over the place, and Polish flags flew at half mast, together with a piece of concentration camp pyjamas hoisted at the main gate. Barricades barred entry and a crowd of around 150 awaited our arrival. They refused to accept the food deliveries. They refused to allow vehicles to enter. Hugh was inside the Camp already, as he had gone there before breakfast to try and prevent trouble. Lilian and I came back from Siegfriedstrasse after breakfast, having called for the Polish liaison officer, and we left our vehicles outside the Camp. Michael had gone to Bad Harzburg the previous day for 72 hours leave, and I had taken over his duties as Works and Accommodation Officer. Every morning there was a labour parade, at nine o'clock, so we went across the road from our billets towards the Camp. I must admit my heart was in my mouth. We walked purposefully towards the crowd, and greeted them with 'Good morning!' in the Polish tongue. I met my secretary/interpreter, and it became clear we were not going to be able to hold any labour parade and assign duties. I decided to carry on as normal, so far as possible. We knew there was bad feeling abroad since the visit of the Military Police, and that some of the strikers were armed. Lilian came through the crowd and entered the Camp on her own unhindered, and we decided to distribute Red Cross parcels to the expectant mothers, as had been arranged the previous day. Hugh and I went out to fetch the ambulance which contained the parcels. Those on the gate agreed that we could enter the Camp with the parcels, but when we got inside, the crowd became angry and stopped us and forced us to unload into the Gatehouse Guard Room. Hugh left the vehicle at the side of the road. The strikers asked us to move it outside. "Damned if I will", said Hugh, and I agreed with him. The next thing we knew barricades were placed round the ambulance. But at lunch-time our Polish mechanic drove the ambulance out into the main road and parked it for us without being asked. It was, so far as we were concerned, a friendly strike. Beth and Jane, who at this time were working as Welfare Officers in the Siegfried Kaserne, arrived at the gate during the morning and sought entrance, being quite unaware of what was going on. They were politely turned away, and equally politely left. She comments that "we all behaved beautifully and of course the strikers were fully justified in their demands".

We managed to distribute the Red Cross parcels. Members of the Quaker team were eventually allowed free access in and out of the Camp. It was very different from the position at the Heinrich der Loewe Camp. There were no complaints against us, and that was clearly demonstrated.

What were the complaints? A manifesto was prepared setting out five demands:-
1) news about early repatriation to Poland;
2) more food and better quality food;
3) more clothing, especially for the ex-concentration camp inmates;
4) soap;
5) a better attitude on the part of the authorities towards the Polish displaced persons, and not to show more favour towards the German population than the Poles.

It was the ex-concentration camp inmates who were at the root of the trouble. Large notices were displayed : "Monte Casino, Narwik, Tobruk" where Polish troops had fought bravely - "Auschwitz, Dachau, Belsen" - where so many had starved and perished. We strongly sympathised with the complaints. I was tempted to put up a banner outside our porch. On the second day a General from 30 Corps and four officers came to receive the complaints, and a delegation of five from the Camp went to see him. They were well satisfied with the result, and on the third day, the banners and barricades were taken down, the Polish flag flew at the top of the flag-pole once more, and the General promised a second visit. Better food was promised, and it was anticipated that the first transport of Poles could be leaving within five weeks.

In the midst of this crisis came news that Michael and Lilian were to go on leave. Michael arrived back from Bad Harzburg at lunch-time on the Friday only to leave with Lilian for Belsen by 4 p.m., where they were to stay the night before proceeding to Brussels, and a train from there to Ostend on Sunday. After the sea crossing overnight, they would arrive in England on the Monday morning. This was the pattern with leave travel arrangements. Many experienced long delays at different points in the journey. From this time forward we went on leave in pairs for eleven days at a time. Mine was one of the last in the list and I had to wait till October.

A better spirit prevailed in the Camp during the following weeks. But while Lilian and Michael were away on leave we had a difficult time. The Army delivered a transport of Poles to the Camp before we had time to prepare room for them. About six hundred came, and we had been preparing to receive three hundred. We were expecting them to arrive on the Wednesday and Friday, but the came on Thursday as well! By this time we had 2820 persons resident in the Camp, now known as 'The Quaker Centrum'. They lived in eleven barrack squares of blocks of buildings. Many had families. Almost all were unresponsive and ungrateful, I remarked in a letter. At times we were very despondent about our role, the shortages of resources, and the lack of news for the Poles about their futures which provided a tense atmosphere.

There were moments of relaxation and leisure. One night we enjoyed a splendidly professional Revue put on by the Radan Theatre Group, a Polish displaced persons concert party which toured the camps entertaining. They returned a little later and gave us a second show, called appropriately "Topsy-Turvy!" which just about summed up our lives at this time.

In the main our lives remained rather dull and depressing, - all the dis - words came to mind in describing it, such as disappointing and dissatisfying. But there were periods of intense activity, and some excitements.

I describe one day as a particularly tough day because we were to have a visit from the General again, so I started by getting the thirteen labourers to tidy up the Camp. Also we discovered that people had been burning the brand new wooden beds we put up in Block 1 for fuel, so we had to go round nailing all the doors up, chalking on the outside the number of places available, ready for the next arrivals. Hugh asked me to fetch the cigarettes for the Camp employees, this being one form of payment for labour. These were two weeks overdue. I was reluctant to leave my duties, and in the end the Polish liaison officer went in my place. A teacher for the school had arrived, and since she was a single woman this presented an accommodation problem, no single rooms being available. I was informed that Room 224 Block 1 was empty, and when I inspected it, in place of the empty rubbish strewn across the warped floor which I had expected, I found three inhabitants comfortably ensconced in a truly beautiful room. So finally I found accommodation for her elsewhere. The next task was to visit the kitchen, where there were problems about the milk supply : too little was delivered and it was going sour. Joyce and I investigated and then we went to see the wholesale supplier. The cigarettes arrived and I distributed them to our twenty-five labourers. Then I went to the Royal Engineers (D.C.R.E.) to see if they could come and repair our Camp refrigerator to stop the milk going sour. Following a row with the cleaner in the Out-patients Department about the standard of his work, I received the news that all the German cleaners at our flats had given notice. The Polish liaison officer then asked me to collect the luggage of a man who had just been released from prison. But he didn't appear at the place where I was waiting for him. In between all these various tasks, I managed to complete some office work, compiling lists, returns, figures. What a day!

Michael returned from leave and I was very glad to hand over to him so that he could resume his duties, which I had taken over in his absence. Hugh and Lyn went on leave next, so I took over Hugh's duties as Commandant of Gypsy Camp for the two weeks he was away. I thought it would be simply a case of "holding the baby" in his absence, but I was gravely mistaken. During his absence we had one of the greatest crises I had ever experienced. Hugh left in a plane from the Camp at Gypsy, where the grass runways of the aerodrome still remained serviceable, and had been used by French and Belgian pilots to land planes to collect their fellow countrymen and fly them home. They used some hangars in a remote part of the airfield, and we had no connection with this operation. Hugh flew with a party of Americans to Brussels. There was one occasion when a strange aircraft landed and I took the ambulance and my secretary/interpreter to find out what was going on. It turned out to be an American pilot who was lost on his way back from a weekend in Berlin. We arranged for him to refuel and have some refreshment, then he took off after expressing his deep gratitude.

The first task after Hugh's departure was to arrange for the introduction of a new ration scheme. This involved centralisation of the warehouse from which the food was to be collected in the Hermann Goehring Works a distance of some ten kilometres away from us, at 7.30 each morning. The Army were in charge of that place, not the Germans, which was a source of some satisfaction to the displaced persons. We also received some UNRRA stores and food from the American Lend-Lease scheme, which meant more variety could be provided in the diet. But in order to collect the food we had to prepare indents and take a Bedford 15-cwt truck and the three-ton lorry to fetch it, leaving Gypsy Camp at 7 in the morning.

There is a story attached to this ration-collecting chore. At 6.45 a.m. one wintry morning it was my turn to drive the three-tonner to collect the rations. I went across to the Camp kitchens to collect the kitchen workers who accompanied us on these occasions, reversing the vehicle carefully into the bay so that they could embark. As I drove off I took a wide turn across the road and to the left over the adjoining barrack square. My windscreen was misted over and the wipers did not clear the part at the extreme left side, and I completely forgot there was a fire-hydrant right on the edge of this parade ground. I demolished it and burst the radiator of the three-tonner, rendering it unserviceable. I had to hastily arouse some Team members to drive other vehicles to fetch the rations, and anxiously watched as the flood from the hydrant spread all over the square and eventually into the basements where there were some residents. We could not turn off the water supply until the German Camp foreman Willi arrived for work at 7.45 a.m. Imagine my embarrassment. There is no mention of this incident in any surviving letters home!

To continue, we suddenly received an order to move 600 men from the Camp. This involved a considerable amount of organisation. At this time, we were informed of a re-organisation of the Polish Guard, which provided a uniformed guard service to the Camp. They were to be withdrawn to their headquarters in central Brunswick, leaving us without a guard. Strenuous efforts by several team members and the Polish liaison officer lasted till 2.30 a.m. before we gained a reprieve. At 11.30 that night the lorries had arrived to collect the Polish Guard. The Sergeant in charge, a very good friend of the team, came to see me to ask what was to be done. We were unwilling to leave the Camp unguarded, especially that night. Michael went with him to our Military Government officers, after receiving the advice of the local Major M., who lived in one of the adjoining flats. From 822 Mil.Gov. they went to the Polish liaison officer, thence to the Polish Major, and to the Polish Captain in the Polish barracks. In the end the order was cancelled at 2 a.m. and they returned triumphantly to Gypsy Camp at 2.30 a.m.

On the very same day we received a bombshell - the news that the whole Gypsy Camp was to be evacuated and the population moved to Sande, near Wilhelmshafen on the North Sea coast. This was Tuesday. It was not until the following Friday that this move was cancelled, after we had made strenuous efforts to forestall it. Beth, Bill B. and I had visited the Headquarters of 30 Corps 5th Division to make representations, and the Polish liaison officers had done their utmost to prevent the move. When news of the reprieve came after four days of nightmare existence I nearly broke down with relief, and we paused to recover our breath. But this news did not reach us before we had planned to move 3000 persons the following Monday, with preparations for a two-day journey, and made arrangements to place the sick in hospital, and to provide for the needs of those who were weak through ill-health but who would be travelling with the party, as well as for the mothers with babies.

When I met the blockleaders to give them the good news, accompanied by the Polish liaison officer who announced it, the congratulations were profuse and sincere. Each blockleader came to shake my hand most warmly. Nobody had thought it possible we could change the Army's plan to move these unfortunate folk to the other end of occupied Germany in order to place British troops in our camp. The impossible had happened!

By this time I was eagerly anticipating my turn for leave. A long journey home was involved, as follows:
1) by car to Hannover;
2) by train to Ostend, taking 22 hours, commencing at midnight;
3) by ship to Tilbury;
4) a night in London;
5) train home, after reporting at Friends House, the headquarters of the Friends Relief Service.

It would only be eleven days leave, and there would not be sufficient time for me to visit Liverpool and Aberystwyth, as I would have liked. One could not be sure how long the journey would take. Hugh had been delayed two days at Ostend waiting for a passage, and one night in Brussels, so leaving Brunswick on a Saturday afternoon he was not in London till the following Wednesday. Lyn on her return journey took six days (or five nights). But Michael, leaving on Friday evening, had arrived in London on the Monday evening. One could never be sure. My parents were anxious to meet me in London but I dissuaded them on account of the uncertainty.

My leave passed well but all too quickly, and before you could say 'Jack Robinson' I was on my way back. I left my luggage at Fenchurch Street Station, London, while I had a meal with my Uncle Baldwyn and visited the London Welsh Club. I only just caught the 9.41 p.m. train to Purfleet, where we were met by three troop-carrying vehicles. Into the back of a truck I climbed, in the dark with twenty other fellows, and after a bumpy five-mile journey, we arrived at a transit camp under canvas. There were five groups of tents, each named after a General, thus : Wavell Lines, Alexander Lines, Montgomery Lines. Each had separate accommodation for Officers, Warrant Officers and Sergeants, and Other Ranks. As a person having "officer" status I was escorted to a tent where there were eight beds, one occupied by a sleeping figure. I collected four blankets from the store. I was asked if I had eaten and said I had had a snack. I was shown in the Officer's Mess and sat down to an enormous meal of sausage meat and chips and a pint mug of tea with plenty of sugar! I slept soundly till 7.45 a.m. when the orderly brought me a mug of tea! Breakfast was cooked ham and fried potatoes, tea, and bread and jam. There followed a long wait. We were informed we would be sailing in the afternoon. The Camp boasted a cinema, church and barber's shop as well as a comfortable Officer's Mess situated in an old manor house. This was now full of very bored looking officers of every description. There was a middle-aged official from UNRRA, a Military Government officer, a group of specialist/technicians from the Allied Control Commission, Reconnaissance, the Cameron Highlanders, the Dorset regiment, Polish Officers, Belgian Flying Officers, one sailor, what a strange collection, I thought as I sat in front of a roaring fire and wrote letters. A radio burbled ineffectively in one corner. Some played cards. Some were reading. There was some noise at the bar.

The call to report for our transport came at 3 p.m. on Monday afternoon, and we sailed about 6 p.m. for Ostend, arriving in time for a late breakfast the following morning. The ship was a large two-funneller which used to ply the Irish Sea. It was very full, and I was put in with 72 officers to sleep in one large cabin three decks down, with very little room or ventilation. I soon decided to seek a more comfortable resting place, and ended up curled up on deck in a cosy spot on a pile of ropes. I slept from 10.30 till 5.00 a.m. At Ostend, after breakfast at the Red Cross hostel, I did some shopping, purchasing a thermos flask (which I broke on the train), some electrical plugs, sewing machine needles, blackboard dusters, dishcloths, etc. I caught the train at 6.40 p.m. on Tuesday evening, and had a two-bunk sleeping compartment which I shared with an Intelligence Officer. We had breakfast in Wesel, and early dinner (or late lunch) at Minden at 3 p.m., arriving in Hannover at 5 p.m. I phoned Brunswick, and at 9 p.m. Bill B. called for me, and we got back to Gypsy Camp at 10 p.m. to find my room re-arranged and a fire and hot bath to greet me, which was very welcome, as I had picked up a cold, probably due to the damp and muddy conditions at Purfleet. Then I caught up with all the news.

The big news concerned the first departure to Poland. On the Saturday after I left on my leave the Major came and called a conference to announce that 1000 should leave the next day. At 10 p.m. everyone started work preparing for the departure. The administrative staff worked until 3.00 a.m. and my office workers until 5.00 a.m. preparing lists of people, filling in the required Displaced Persons cards, and arranging all the details. At 2.00 p.m. the next day the lorries started moving off with their human cargo, a process which lasted till 6 p.m. Food was provided in boxes for each lorry-load of twenty-two persons. Everyone was medically examined before leaving, and the Polish liaison officer asked each person whether they wanted to go to Poland. It proved difficult to raise the required number. The first check showed no more than 500 being willing to go, but in the end 797 people left. Reports of the journey showed that they were well cared for en route, and that everything was well organised and arranged. At the Polish border there were no less than thirteen separate security checks.

That same evening, Sunday, 275 new arrivals came into our Camp from a neighbouring town, Watenstedt, which was ten miles away. They had not been expected till the next day. It was an unwelcome end to a hectic forty-eight hours. Eventually all officers and staff staggered to their beds at about nine or ten that Sunday night.

Otherwise there was little news. Our Team Leader Lyn was now at 30 Corps Headquarters as British Red Cross Liaison Officer temporarily. A new team member David J. had arrived and was settling in. Blankets had been distributed in the Camp and clothing for the ex-concentration camp folk. A row developed about the arrangements for distributing Red Cross parcels.

On the first day after my return 94 people arrived in lorries from the camp at Rote Wiese, which was being used as a collection point for people from the villages and farms. When sufficient people had gathered there they were transported to Gypsy Camp. They arrived with piles of bug-infested mattresses, cupboards and beds. I immediately got the three-tonner loaded up and deposited all these in an empty garage. We had no DP registration cards or food cards, so Hugh went off to the store we had established soon after our arrival in Brunswick in a disused air-raid shelter on the outskirts of the city to see what he could find which would serve these purposes. The new arrivals had to wait meanwhile before we could register and powder them. In the afternoon I took a delegation with two large wreaths to a Roman Catholic cemetery. The previous day the Poles had been mourning those who died in the concentration camps. After a Team meeting in the afternoon I returned to the garage to supervise the storage of more bug-infested cupboards, which were to be disinfested the following day. After supper we all had to turn our hands to unpacking the Red Cross parcels. These had to be broken down into their components ready for distribution the following day. This rule had been adopted in order to prevent any black market in whole parcels. The Army had ordered that all the foodstuffs in the parcels should go to the Camp kitchen, the rest of the contents, such as cigarettes, soap, chewing gum, etc. was to be distributed on a daily basis over a period of a fortnight, so that each person would get the equivalent of a whole parcel every two weeks. This was the second or third distribution we had made, but previous distributions had been made before the rule about breaking down the parcels had been introduced. Moreover, previously the distribution had been made only to those who were sick, pregnant mothers and school children, and we knew that the promise of parcels for each and every one of the Camp residents would cause difficulties over distribution.

So at nine in the evening on Thursday five members of the team, after completing a day's work, started to open the parcels and sort their contents. The Camp blockleaders had refused to have anything to do with the scheme (a) because they disapproved of the breaking down of the parcels (b) because they were afraid of being accused of dishonesty. "Only the Quakers must do this", they said, and our commandant Hugh had agreed we should do it at least on the first occasion. By 1.00 a.m. we had done no more than 500 parcels out of 3000. We told the Blockleaders and the Military Government that it was impossible to undertake such an immense task and we felt that the Poles should be made to undertake some responsibility for this themselves. By 1.00 a.m. we were very tired and very depressed. That was my first supposedly quiet day back at work after my leave.

The next morning began with hundreds of people surging to Hugh's office to protest about the situation. Somehow they had the idea that the Blockleaders had agreed to "their" parcels being opened and broken down according to their contents. A few irresponsible and partially drunk hooligans beat up the Camp Elder or chief Blockleader and he arrived at Hugh's office dazed and bleeding profusely from a nasty head-wound. Another Blockleader was severely mauled, and some of the Blockleaders' rooms were wrecked. The Military Government Major arrived and addressed a meeting. He told them that the scheme of distribution was being carried out by us on his instructions, which he had received from higher quarters. He was rather outspoken to begin with but later modified his position and promised to speak to the General about the situation. The meeting broke up amid scenes of disorder.

The Camp Elder resigned from his position and his work as Blockleader, but with the intervention of Hugh, who brought in the priest, he was reinstated by the people themselves and agreed to continue to serve. Another Blockleader was thrown out in no uncertain manner.

To complicate matters, we learned that the Military had chosen that night to make a detailed check on the whereabouts of everyone in the Camp after curfew. It is not recorded whether there were any further complaints and protests as a result.

The following week came a further transport of 1500 to Poland. We were asked to send 400 from Gypsy Camp and given 48 hours notice. With my staff I started to compile lists, to ensure that each person possessed a Displaced Person's Card, that we had a duplicate, and that each person underwent a medical examination. We were mainly looking for typhus, typhoid and infectious diseases. Then we arranged them in groups of twenty, and they assembled in the Camp cinema so that the Polish liaison officer could issue each one with a visa. We worked from 9 a.m. till 11 p.m. and throughout the following day, when we expected the lorries to collect the people and take them to the station at Brunswick. Only two of the expected twelve lorries arrived, which hampered the arrangements a bit, but by 6.30 p.m. the last person was on the train, which had been due to leave at 5.30 p.m. It left two hours late. The people were in cold unheated freight vans but it was not a long journey to Luneburg, where they were to stay the night. The next day lorries would pick them up and take them on a two-day journey via Dessau and Stettin to Poland. The Polish authorities would receive them at Stettin.

Following this transport on the Friday we received notification of another scheduled for the following Tuesday. This notice arrived on Saturday. On Sunday morning Hugh collected lists from the Blockleaders of those who wished to go. There were about 70, so we asked for places for 100 on the train. Jane, Beth and Kit informed those who were still living in private accommodation in the western part of the area, since they had been under our care for some time and were our responsibility. On Monday we collected the Displaced Persons papers in my office together with the duplicates for those who were leaving, and once again we went through the screening, visa and medical procedures.

On Tuesday, the day of the departure of this transport, my duty was to meet the lorries outside our Military Government offices in Siegfriedstrasse and escort them to Gypsy Camp, and supervise the loading of the lorries, twenty persons to each one, to collect and distribute Red Cross parcels, one for each person, and accompany the first vehicle down to the Station in order to hand over the papers to the Polish liaison officer there, who accompanied the party all the way. The duplicates were sent to the Headquarters of the British Army of The Rhine (B.A.O.R.) who would then transmit them to the Polish Government.

On both these transports I judged the arrangements which we, the Quaker Relief Team, had made to be well-nigh perfect, and that nobody could accuse us of overlooking any detail. This could hardly be said of the military. On the first occasion they turned up with only one-sixth of the lorries we had expected. On the second occasion, after we had confirmed all the details of the arrangements at a Conference at the Military Government HQ, the station was changed at the last moment without notifying us. The result was that I turned up at the wrong station with two lorry-loads of Poles, and the drivers discharged their human cargo and returned to Gypsy Camp. There followed a wait of one and a half hours before two lorries came to carry us to Brunswick *East* Station. There was little liaison between the Military Government and the Railway Officers. Forty Poles, including women and children were left stranded in an empty station in bitterly cold weather, simply because no-one

Repatriation to Poland, the train comes into the camp

had thought fit to notify us of the last-minute change in the station. Of course, being the man on the spot I was the one who was blamed!

Now we were given to understand that there would be no further transports to Poland until the Spring. There was talk of new arrangements for transporting 8000 Poles a week by sea in December, and we feared we would be required to find people willing to travel. Not many people wished to travel at this time of the year, and we thought it would be difficult to fill any quota allotted to us. There was talk of forcing them to go, and we foresaw trouble ahead.

Roger Wilson, the General Secretary of FRS at Friends House, had been visiting Germany, as Travelling Commissioner for the Friends Relief Service, accompanied by a 'weighty Friend' who was seeking to renew Quaker contacts in Germany. There was some discussion about the plans for the future of our Team and the other two FRS Teams in the area. We thought we would stay till the Spring at least. Some members who had been on a six-month's engagement had signed up for a further period. Michael and I told Roger we would be prepared to move elsewhere at this stage and leave our work to be done by others, but when we learned that the only vacancy would be as transport drivers in Cologne, we felt it would be better to remain over the winter in Brunswick, when we thought that conditions in Germany might deteriorate and some more demanding relief work might be required of us.

It was at this time that I busied myself helping to start a Camp Cobblers Shop. This involved getting the agreement of the five staff to the terms and conditions of work and pay, as well as ensuring a supply of tools and materials. [A copy of the Cobblers Workshop agreement with the Camp administration survives.]

I took a Sunday off to visit my old school friend Stanley whom I had met by such a strange chance in Ostend. He was now in Hamburg, and although I was unable to give him advance notice of my visit, I was lucky to find him free for the afternoon. The journey there was interesting, as we crossed the Luneburg Heath where the German forces surrendered to the Allied Forces the previous May on terms laid down by General Montgomery. It was a wilderness of pine trees and heathland with the roads running straight across. Apart from the towns of Uelzen and Luneburg, we passed through only villages, but those towns impressed us with their beauty. The New Statesman had recently described how a newspaper had been restarted in Luneburg. Passing through the southern suburbs of Hamburg, we saw only about twenty inhabitable houses, and the destruction was awesome to behold. It was not a scene of total destruction, however, such as I had seen in Munster and Osnabruck. Bare walls stood everywhere without roof or floor or windows, the result of the 'blockbuster' bombing raids we had heard about. We had seen the honeycomb effect shown in aerial photographs. We drove through miles of gutted houses, flats, and warehouses and factories, and it was difficult to see where people could be living. Yet, according to the figures we had seen, the population of three million having fallen to one-and-a-half million after the bombing, had risen again since, with the addition of refugees from the east and displaced persons, until it had now reached two million. Later I read in the paper that the current population of Hamburg was 1,350,000, whereas before the war it had been 1,700,000. Since the end of the war the population had risen by 25,000 a month, 300,000 altogether, and daily there were new arrivals. As Stanley remarked, the big question was, where were they all living and on what? In the centre of the city, large blocks of offices and hotels remained unscathed, as if part of the plan, and these limited facilities were now occupied by the Allied forces, who enjoyed the comfort of the best accommodation available.

Back at Gypsy Camp, following the departure of the transports to Poland, it was decided to move the remainder of the Displaced Persons in the Landkreis or County into Gypsy Camp. This meant much work for me in the familiar role of Reception Officer, arranging the registration, powdering and medical checks, together with a typhus injection, for each person on arrival. The doctor who did those injections also handed out the food card, and in this way we prevented evasion of the injection. Many displaced persons were afraid of having injections after what they had seen and heard about lethal injections during the Nazi period.

It was now a year since the Team had come together in Friends House, London, to hear about the invitation to take part in the relief work in Europe as members of Relief Team RT/100 FRS. We were all proud to have had this opportunity. I recounted how I had heard one little man wishing he were in a Quaker Camp rather than one run by UNRRA. We ourselves thought there was a qualitative difference and this may well have been the case.

We were also quite comfortable in our new quarters. Not only did we now have a separate Mess in the flat above the one which we occupied, but we had our own garages and a number of mechanics drawn from the Camp population to service and repair our vehicles. The snow had now fallen, and was lying six inches thick on the ground. To keep warm we had to retire early to bed. I now had a staff of six, and we expected another transport to be arranged quite soon, to travel by sea from Lubeck to Poland.

Jane had been distributing knitting wool for the women and children in the Camp and clothes for the men. There were no knitting needles, and the following morning many bicycles in the Camp seemed to have lost some spokes from their wheels! One consequence of the absence of needles was that the wool did not go so far because the garments knitted on the bicycle spokes were very fine gauge which took more wool! We had come to the end of the Red Cross parcels by this time. The Cobblers Shop was running smoothly, and I was now making plans to open a Tailors' Workshop and Store. Many Christmas parties were being planned, and Michael and I went to buy toys to distribute as presents, one for each child. Later on we actually had a toymakers workshop in the Camp.

In the Camp there was talk of an underground movement fighting against the Russians in Poland, in the forests and the mountains, and about one hundred of our ex-concentration camp inmates were waiting for the Russians to leave Warsaw before returning. They were busy making detailed plans to sweep the communists from power and establish democratic government. This proved much more difficult than any of them imagined, and it took another forty years or more to achieve democracy in Poland. I discussed with returning relief workers who had experience of working in the east zone the behaviour of the Russians as occupying forces. They had some horrific stories to tell. At this time a correspondence appeared in a Welsh language weekly paper 'Y Faner', in which an Army officer who had had the same kind of experiences challenged the cosy apologia which had appeared there for the Russians' behaviour, and gave chapter and verse of atrocities and misbehaviour. In my discussions with the relief workers we agreed that the Army officer's version was nearer to the truth. [This correspondence was the result of a letter which I wrote to George M.Ll. Davies which was printed in 'Y Faner' and which is reproduced in Appendix 6.]

Lyn had now left the Team permanently to become the British Red Cross Liaison Officer in the Displaced Persons Control at 30 Corps. There was talk of Hugh going to work in France with his wife Juanita in Toulouse, but this did not transpire; instead she came to join our Team and work in Gypsy Camp. We chose to nominate Hugh as the new Team Leader, which seemed natural since he was the Commandant of Gypsy Camp and led our eight Team members working there. Bill B. had too much responsibility by this time as Senior Medical Officer in the 822 Mil.Gov Detachment. Some rearrangement of our tasks was undertaken, since several Team members would be leaving in February. Others would stay till April, which was when the arrangement between the Red Cross and UNRRA expired. Beth was going to Poland, Marjorie would be leaving quite soon, but Diana M. came to join us from

Cologne, and other women were expected from London. A relative newcomer to the Team David J., who was a Friend, became Deputy Leader.

By this time I had moved into a new office with my secretary/interpreter which we shared with Michael, leaving five staff in the old office adjacent. Michael brought with him his work as the person in charge of Buildings and Labour, and I was trying to develop the workshops and stores, as well as helping Michael over sanitation.

Another hundred new arrivals from the farms and villages had to be accommodated. They suffered a considerable decline in their living standards by coming into the Camp. They had lived like lords since the liberation, and had done no work.

The fourth transport to Poland left early in December, consisting of 118 persons. They were taken in lorries to Luneburg, thence by train to Lubeck, and from there by sea to Gdynia. The party included one mother with a six-months' old baby as well as a seventy-year old woman.

We had two typhoid cases in December, which caused quite a panic; all sorts of precautions ensued. The sanitation system was completely scrubbed clean. We had 20,000 doses of typhoid vaccine ready.

Each Camp resident received two Red Cross parcels in December. The only real problem was the supply of coal. We had received twice the normal allocation in November, collecting this ourselves for the two months till the end of the year. .Then the arrangements were altered and the military were to deliver the coal. The result was we were without central heating in the Camp for two weeks. The School and Nursery School had to be shut. But on 15th December twelve lorry loads of coal arrived.

Things were getting difficult in other ways. The military had let it be known that those who did not return to Poland would not have any priority in future with regard to food and general supplies. The Red Cross parcels were now regarded as part of the food ration. Requisitioning in the town had ceased to be possible, and there was much unrest and uncertainty in the Camp.

Before embarking on the hectic round of parties and celebrations at Gypsy Camp over the Christmas period, I enjoyed a 72-hour break at Bad Harzburg. Here I was accommodated in the large and rambling spa hotel, the Harzburger Hof. Here I ate like a lord, enjoying a four-course lunch and seven-course dinner. A tea dance was held in the afternoon, a Variety Show in the evening. Friday was spent learning to ski on a beginner's slope about 3000 feet up in the Harz mountains, where there was about a metre of snow. We were a party of seven officers and we had a very tall German instructor. Some rocks and bracken showed through the snow, and we tried to avoid them. We spent the whole day on the slopes in brilliant sunshine, lunching in the near-by German Sports House (a bowl of soup, lemonade, sandwiches, cake and tea). A dance in the hotel that night proved disappointing, however. The next morning was again spent on the ski slopes, then after lunch we set off on a tramp (lang-laufen) and found a few suitable slopes to fall on and many ditches to fall in. That night we attended a Night Club called the Barberina where there was a cabaret show (something I had never seen before).

It was with great reluctance that we returned to Gypsy Camp on Sunday morning. Early on Monday morning we received a great shock. Our sleeping accommodation overlooked the Camp entrance. There the Polish armed guard checked the arrivals and departures. Each displaced person was supposed to show his papers. As I was putting my sleeping bag over the window-sill, a man cycled out of the Camp without showing his papers. The Polish guard immediately called upon him to halt and dismount. The man ignored the shout and cycled on. The guard fired a warning shot in the air. The man continued on his way. Then the soldier took aim and shot the cyclist through the head and killed him. I called on Beth to come with me at once and calmly told her a man had been shot while trying to leave the Camp, just as quietly as if I was asking her the time, it seems. I arranged for undertakers to be called. In our billets, Beth comforted the deceased man's wife and mother with endless cups of sweet tea and fresh handkerchiefs. It seems that the deceased had only been married a few weeks. Thankfully Hugh arrived before I had to arrest the soldier responsible who was detained by the Camp police in the guard-house. We both attended the funeral later in the week, and I took thirty people with me in the three-tonner. A few months later I attended the soldier's trial for manslaughter before the German Criminal Court in Brunswick, which as a law graduate interested in criminal law and procedure fascinated me. I was particularly interested to observe the inquisitorial mode of trial. As I recall the soldier was sent to prison for three years for manslaughter.

In the afternoon of the shooting incident I attended the Children's Christmas Party. There was a crib, and the choir sang carols. Santa Claus appeared and gave each child a present (which Michael and I had bought earlier out of Camp monies). There were dolls, whirligigs, yo-yo's, balancing clowns, pull-string cut-outs, model villages and farms, and paint-boxes. Everybody had cocoa and cake. There were twenty cream cakes at the start and nothing left at the end! There was a Carol Service, where inevitably the atmosphere was rather sad at first because of the shooting, and when the lights failed that seemed to be the last straw. But miraculously candles were produced and lit and the spirits rose and the singing swelled and by the end everyone was feeling much better!

Many more parties took place that evening, followed by a Midnight Mass in the chapel which was packed to the doors. This was a very moving experience, being the first Christmas since the liberation, and with the Poles facing so many uncertainties as to the future. A small party was hosted by the Blockleaders in the evening, when they presented Hugh with a camera. On Christmas morning the Team foregathered with senior Camp officials for coffee and cake, and Hugh made a little speech (in Polish!). Presents were given to those from the Camp.

The Cobblers made a most remarkable Christmas tree, using the materials from their workshop, nails, leather soles and the like. One of my pre-Christmas duties was to make a tour of inspection of all the basements in the Camp, accompanied by the police chief and a guard, in order to seek out illicit stills, and when they were found, confiscate them. We could usually tell by the smell of spirits being distilled. It was quite dangerous to make spirits from potatoes and other such ingredients, since it could cause blindness, and there had been some deaths. I remember well being courteously received at one suspect basement where the residents offered us a glass of what was described as black-currant wine, which we accepted since it was a cold night! After that we could hardly confiscate their hidden vodka, so we turned on our heels and left, with many felicitations for the Christmas season. On one such search of the basements Joyce found a man who was breeding mice in cages in order to make a fur coat for his wife. These mice had a stripe along the spine which made them attractive, at least to him!

In the afternoon of Christmas Day we went to the forest to collect fuel. This was not just a token gathering of the Yule log, for we had insufficient fuel to ensure cooking breakfast the following morning! We had our Christmas Dinner at 822 Mil.Gov. with turkey and plum pudding, after which we attended a Dance at Gypsy Camp which lasted until the early hours, but I left at two in the morning. This was just as well, because on Boxing Day morning I was awakened at nine a.m. by the nurse who asked me to take a patient to hospital. In the afternoon I carried the visiting football team, which had beaten Gypsy Camp 3-1, back to their Camp at Watenstedt, twelve miles away. As I returned to rejoin our Team members at the theatre, hoping to enjoy the amateur theatre party show, I was unlucky to be intercepted by the nurse with another urgent hospital case. That night I hosted a party for my office staff, all six of them. Joyce and Michael came to help by speaking German, and we had coffee and cake, and I gave them each a present. This was the first time I had ever hosted a party! The men each received a handkerchief containing shaving soap, razor blades, toothpaste, a toothbrush, soap, boot-polish and elastoplast. These were all items in short supply. The girls each received a scarf containing appropriate toiletries.

The following weekend, after I had collected oranges, chocolate and sugar from the Polish Red Cross store in Brunswick on the Saturday, I worked all day Sunday on the task of preparing fresh food cards for everyone in the Camp, bearing their name and address, which had to be ready by Monday morning. We filled in over 1,000 cards.

About this time we learned with some alarm that there was a plot to assassinate our Camp Commandant Hugh, for unknown reasons. A Polish prisoner in the Brunswick gaol claimed to have overheard some other prisoners discussing it. (Hugh and I have a copy of the statement he made.) Naturally security precautions were upgraded and life became for a while a little more difficult for us all. My letters give some details of the precautions taken to protect the Team. On New Year's Eve we all attended a dance at 822 Mil.Gov. Twenty-four British soldiers were on guard outside, and one officer provided a personal escort for Hugh. The Major at 822 Mil.Gov. announced at the beginning of the party that no-one was to leave until the end, and that we were surrounded by an armed guard with orders to shoot on sight! At Gypsy Camp the guard of Polish police was augmented to 70 Polish guards. New Year's Eve or any night until January 7th had been mentioned in our warning, and none of us slept very easily until that period passed.

It seems that we visited the German cinema quite frequently during the winter months, finding the programmes there much more interesting and to our liking than the British Army cinema. For example, early in January I saw a soccer match between England and Wales, and some report of the Belsen war crimes trials, which had now begun. Our secretary/interpreters accompanied us on this occasion, and they recognised the infamous commandant from Belsen, Kramer, Irme Grese (the beast of Belsen, as she was called in the popular press), and a woman called Bormann, each of whom they had known in Belsen.

A new woman member of the Team had now arrived from London, Beryl W., who eventually became Team Leader. I remarked that it must be difficult for her to adjust to living in a Team like ours had become in the eleven months we had been together. After all our experiences we must have become a rather strange crew! I was unwilling to leave the Team, however, in February, and resolved to stay at least until April. To leave any earlier would be in my opinion like leaving a house that was on fire when one was in the middle of putting it out! Moreover we were all fearful of the frightful conditions which were extremely likely to occur in the camp and in Germany before the end of the winter months. I preferred to stay at least until the summer and the sunshine returned.

I was at this time exploring the possibilities of gaining admission to Cambridge to study law at the post-graduate level. This had been quite a common practice for good law graduates from my college in Wales, and, though it was hard to believe at times, I had gained a First Class Honours Degree in law at Aberystwyth. I was considering the alternative careers open to me, as a private solicitor, in local government work, or in some helping role such as Poor Man's Lawyer (I had some experience of this work at Cambridge House Camberwell, while I was in London working in the East End, and had discussed it with some of those involved).

Meanwhile things had become more difficult as the winter progressed at Gypsy Camp. The army (30 Corps) introduced an entirely new Ration Scale in the New Year, quite different from anything that went before. Henceforth rations were to be drawn in five categories or more : Adult Normal Consumers, children aged 0-6, 6-19, expectant mothers and nursing mothers, heavy workers, other workers, the sick and disabled. This meant re-organizing the method of food distribution. Whereas previously they had collected three days of dry rations for a whole block, and the individual share-out was done by the blockleaders, and a serving of soup had been made at mid-day to everyone, now we constructed an average out of the five or six new ration scales and distributed this, as before, through the blockleaders, together with mid-day soup, but the extra rations, which in some cases amounted to as much as 1000 calories a day for some workers, were given out in special distributions. We planned to cook a special soup twice a week for the expectant and nursing mothers. The 6-19 year-olds had to get their food three times a day in the Children's Kitchen. Facilities were provided for them to consume the food on the spot if they wished to do so.

Complaints which we faced were (1) that some of the 17 to 19 year-olds did not like queueing up with the 6-8 year-olds; (2) the supply of cigarettes for workers was reduced from 20 a week or a basic ration of 80 per month to 60 a month; (3) there was no butter supply nor fresh meat, only margarine and canned meat.

In addition, a careful check of the numbers in each block had shown that some blockleaders had been seriously overdrawing rations for their block, but getting accurate figures was quite impossible, and arriving at anything like a close approximation nearly drove my office team and myself mad! For example, we found that in the three months since the end of September, despite daily notifications of changes from each blockleader, we had been drawing rations for 200 too many. At this point, early in January 1946, we had 2538 people resident in the Camp.

I had re-organised our General Store under an efficient and reliable storekeeper. We received a delivery of 400 mattresses when we were only expecting 150, which meant that we had to find extra room for storage. The Cobblers Shop was speeding up the rate of production, and everything seemed to be going quite well there, although there had been some complaints about over-charging. I was busy organising a Paint Store and getting a painter to start redecorating the kitchens, and other parts of the Camp, including the railings outside. He also did some notices for us with stencils we managed to procure from 822 Mil.Gov.

A mattress and blanket distribution was carried out by Jane, and 100 men were also supplied with clothing. Joyce had come out of hospital, where she had been with some infection or swelling of the foot. Lilian was detained in hospital rather longer with quite a serious illness. Joyce managed to track down a German woman abortionist, with the help of the Camp doctor, a German, and together they visited her address to verify it, then called the police. The woman was now safely in jail on remand. Joyce has some vivid impressions of this German doctor and the two German nurses who were working at the Camp hospital by this time, who she recollects as being rather authoritarian in their approach. She also remembers how difficult it was to prevent the Camp children from queueing up twice to receive their cod-liver oil - they had been so used to shortages and cheating in queues!

Beth was winding up her work with the displaced persons living in private accommodation in our area (the Guides Team took over this responsibility from us in mid-January). She had worked long and hard with these people from a bleak office in down-town Brunswick, and recalls that the windows had been shattered by the bombing and the glass replaced by paper. There was snow on the ground, and at first practically no heating was provided. In these circumstances she felt entitled to ignore a suggestion contained in a letter from Friends House London that relief staff should beware of being tempted to sit in over-heated offices like the Military personnel at a time when the civilian population was freezing. The Czechs who occupied part of this house soon managed to acquire a supply of coal, however, so that the problem then became one of surviving the over-heated conditions! Shortly afterwards, when these Czechs were due to be repatriated, she was happy to supply a rug which had been donated by her former tutor at LSE to a woman with a very young baby. The journey home would take those people two or three days, and there were fears for the survival of the very young and the elderly in those freezing conditions. Some were known to have died on the way. For a short while Beth was Headmistress of the school in the Camp, and her duties involved shaking every child by the hand each morning as was the Polish custom, and trying to teach English without being able to speak Polish and having only limited amount of German. She was glad to hand over when a qualified Polish teacher arrived. [Beth later went to Poland to continue welfare work.]

We received a delivery of 96 tons of mixed fuel for the month of January. Our camp football team continued its so far unbeaten record in games against local teams from other Camps. We ourselves played hockey regularly with 822 Mil.Gov. against other teams such as the local RAF. I still bear the marks on my leg where our Major struck me, and he was supposed to be on our side!

My Austin ambulance, which had been faithfully serviced and repaired by our two Polish mechanics despite its age, was running well. But at 4 a.m. on 13th January it met its Waterloo. David J. was taking an urgent case to hospital when a car driven by a Polish officer, with another Polish officer and two girl friends as passengers, tore along the road and crashed into the FRS ambulance on a bend, at 50 m.p.h. The driver David, the Polish sister, and the patient were not hurt, but the ambulance was written off as the chassis was bent. Two of the occupants of the small car died and the other two were seriously injured. We received a replacement in due course in the shape of an enormously bulky American Ford ambulance with strangely arranged foot-pedals (not in the usual order but with the brake pedal on the left side of the clutch pedal, which was somewhat disconcerting!).

We continued to hear stories from relief workers who had been working in the Russian zone about the treatment meted out to the local population by the Russians. We were also concerned about conditions in the Ruhr, where, according to reports, severe shortages were making things very difficult. Joyce went to work there with the Red Cross later on and has some interesting accounts of the conditions which she found. A trickle of refugees was arriving from the east continually. For example, a fourteen-year old refugee boy from Poland came into my office one day, saying he had no family and no friends. Then there was the Czech who had lost his father in the fight against the Germans and whose mother was killed by the Russians. He had refused to return to Czechoslovakia with the last transport in January, but according to the Military Government this meant he had to forfeit his status as a Displaced Person and be turned over to the German authorities. There was the Slovak who had married a Ukrainian girl. He claimed he came from the Polish side of the border, and his sister had married a Pole. Not unnaturally he now wished to accompany them both to Poland, but the question was, would he be permitted to do so? There was the case of Adam, the chief clerk in my office staff; he wanted to get married, but the possibility of a civil marriage was denied him, since he could not prove that he had not been married before, and there being no priest from his evangelical church available, he could not have a religious ceremony either. Not surprisingly he was co-habiting.

In musing on these matters, I wrote that it was difficult to know what standards to apply to such situations and such people. How could we judge their behaviour or fault them if at times they acted unreasonably, or proved unreliable. Our own standards were founded on a background of prosperity, plenty and security. The saying that "everything works out well for those who love the Lord" was rather empty of meaning for those who had suffered in Auschwitz, Buchenwald and places like the Hermann Goehring Works at nearby Immendorf. Was it their lack of love of the Lord that had led them to suffer so cruelly in this way? All this time they had kept their faith in freedom and their belief that eventually they would be liberated from oppression. When at last they were freed peace did not bring paradise for them, only seemingly insoluble problems, difficult and even heartbreaking decisions to make, painful and tiresome movements from camp to camp, and the almost superhuman task of assuming responsibility for themselves when they had been driven like machines or sheep for so long. They were not the victors over their problems so much as the problems of the victors!

I quoted from a leading article in The New Statesman of 22nd December 1945:-

"We have never seen any reason to believe that the violent deaths of millions and the social upheavals of continents would produce any kind of Utopia. Why should they? War may end a particular menace, as this one has done : it may sweep away ancient obstructions and release new forces of good and evil. It does not divert the tendencies of history or settle the problems of morality and human relations."

Perhaps this was written by the editor Kingsley Martin, whose memorial service I attended some years later in St. Pancras Church.

The problems in the Camp continued. There was insufficient coal or wood to burn for fuel, the kitchens were in a state of chaos, everything seemed topsy-turvy and working at cross-purposes. There was no-one to say a good word after all our efforts to put things right and hold things together! A Polish Commandant was installed at Gypsy Camp to assist Hugh, but he left after two days, saying he now knew why our hair was prematurely turning grey!

We had been instrumental at this time in helping to set up a German Committee to assist those who as Germans had suffered for their political beliefs. It was an official committee whose purpose, apart from rendering physical aid (and I had supplied a parcel from Wales) was to ensure that priority was given to such people in terms of employment opportunities, and special rations. We had promised to ensure a supply of clothing. As the work with the displaced persons reduced, in the months and years which followed, and after my departure, I understand that the Team turned its attention more and more to the relief of suffering among the German population.

We had great pleasure in attending a performance by the Ballet Rambert in the neighbouring town of Wolfenbuttel. It was a free (ENSA) show, and my first introduction to ballet, and I was enchanted. The beauty of the music combined with the dress and the dancing moved me almost to tears. There was also a Symphony Concert given by the Berlin Philharmonic Orchestra which I attended with great pleasure.

My own morale at this time was pretty low. It seems I had lost my faith in my own personal future as being an orderly progression from one step to the next, from school examinations to college and a degree, to be followed by entering the legal profession. I was like a ship without a rudder, and at a loss about the future, and wondering whether I should stay in Germany for a longer period, possibly by joining UNRRA, or return and undertake graduate studies. We faced daily demands on ourselves and our resources which we found difficult to satisfy. There was no end to the demands made upon us, and I found myself increasingly resistant to meeting some of the more unreasonable ones. One week we were taking pregnant women to the hospital in our ambulance eight times in seven nights. We found the work not only heavy but extremely difficult, with the shortage of resources and the failure of the military to cooperate with the civil authorities, and the presence of UNRRA and the division between the zones in Germany served only to make things worse. Early in February heavy rains caused severe flooding in the centre of Brunswick. Many basements were flooded and businesses ruined under a metre of flood-water. We feared an outbreak of typhoid fever, and more disorganisation and food shortages. For twenty-four hours we were without electricity. The water supply remained intact however. How I longed to sit by a warm fire at home and put these problems behind me!

Suddenly and unexpectedly, I was offered the opportunity to go on leave. It was expected that there would be travel difficulties, since so many of the bridges had been destroyed or damaged by the floods. Fresh transports to Poland had already begun, the first took place in mid-February and another was due soon afterwards, and these affected the date of my leave arrangements. At the end of February 1946 a telegram to my parents announced my arrival date at Harwich and said I expected to be home the following day. I left for Hannover on 24th February, Sunday, hoping to catch a train from there on the Monday morning. This may have been the occasion when, because I was the senior officer travelling, I was asked to be 'train commandant', which meant I was handed the nominal roll of some seven hundred troops on board, and asked to hand it in when we arrived at the Hook of Holland. I was supposedly responsible for ensuring their safe delivery! It had one advantage for me, I was shown into a compartment which I occupied for myself with the blinds drawn, and 'Do no disturb' notices on it, and had a very comfortable journey. The leave passed uneventfully. I met an old school friend who was now an officer in the Army, and another officer friend from College days with whom I had shared lodgings. We went together to Petticoat Lane on the Sunday morning, followed by a good lunch at the Great Eastern Hotel. I left Harwich at 9 p.m., docking in the Hook of Holland about 5.30 a.m. after a good night's sleep. By this time I knew how to organise these things. My train for Hannover left at 9.55 a.m. on the Monday morning, and I expected to be in Hannover by 10.25 p.m. that night, according to my letter home from the Hook of Holland, written the previous evening. After a journey of seven hours through The Netherlands, which gave me an opportunity to see something of the countryside, the canals, villages and towns, we stopped in Bentheim on the German border for a meal. Then on to Hannover via Osnabruck and Minden. I was lucky to find one of the 822 Mil.Gov. officers on the same train and as he had arranged for a car to meet him at Hannover, he kindly offered me a lift. When we arrived there at 10.25 p.m. we were pleased to find the car waiting, and within an hour there was I begging for a bed in the Siegfriedstrasse flats occupied by the Quaker relief workers, to save anyone having to turn out and drive me to the Gypsy Camp at that time of night. Hugh came to fetch me in the morning. After a coffee I went with Hugh to collect his wife Juanita, who had gone to accompany some Camp children to the dentist situated in the Club and Clinic for Displaced Persons which had now been opened in Brunswick, and was run by The Guides Team. We went from there to the Jewish Welfare Club and Canteen for yet another coffee! A new woman member of the Team had arrived from England, Diana P.

On my return I found that all was well. The second transport to Poland had *not* after all left. My staff had done a good job in receiving 288 people from scattered villages around Konigslutter. My office had been painted and decorated in my absence. A message above the door read: "Welcome is Our Old Boss!". Smiles on all sides from the many friends I had made as I traversed the Camp, and many inquiries about my leave and conditions in Britain. My new ambulance had arrived. It was very heavy to drive, but was capable of taking a great many sitting cases. One night I visited the local gaol with some members of the team. We had initiated a regular system of Prison Visits to speak to prisoners in their cells. The gaol at Brunswick was just like any of the Victorian gaols in England. Was this the first time I had visited a prison? Later I wrote three books about prisons and made the subject my own in an academic sense.

When Bill R. went on leave I assumed his responsibilities for pay (which he had taken over from Michael while he was on leave). We busied ourselves with preparing the lists of persons for the impending transport. At the end of this procedure we collected all the people involved (451 of them) in the theatre to be screened and given their visas by the Polish liaison officer. Many of our most trusted and reliable workers left on this occasion, including my chief clerk Adam and two of the filing clerks. After another visit one evening to the German cinema, the next day I briefed the new Accommodation Officer about the difficult task of ensuring that rooms remained intact with their furnishings on the departure of all those people. That night nineteen stragglers were seen by the liaison officer in Hugh's office, and we checked over the Group Lists against the Block Lists, singled out queries and dealt with them. There remained at the end two piles of cards, one pile containing the original DP2 Cards, the other the Duplicate DP2 Cards. One pile numbered 451, the other 454. By a bit of imagination and experience the figure was stabilised at 450, but of course one man did turn up on the morning of the transport. His cards and that of two others had to be stamped at the Station. We had finished work at 11.15 p.m. the previous night.

The stage was set. The German lorries arrived at 7.30 a.m. and by 8.30 sixteen groups of fifteen people had been sent to Brunswick East Station. By 9.45 a.m. the whole 451 had departed. Later that morning we went down to see them in the freight wagons in which they were waiting. It was not until 1 p.m. that they left. The wagons were dirty, one smelt of fish and another of carbide, but this was not unusual. The picture was complete when we found there was no engine, and Captain D. of 822 Mil.Gov. was in a state of much consternation. Major W., his superior, was swanning around in his large limousine. Some of the displaced persons lit a small stove in one of the trucks, which others eventually objected to and kicked right out. Another group had a perforated bucket containing coals which they hung on the door frame like a brazier. Polish flags were placed on the roof of the trucks or pushed out of the slit windows. We were very sorry to see them go, though pleased for them that they were going home!

The Cobblers Shop was going well. I now started a Boys Club with help from the World YMCA. I also was asked to represent Hugh at a Jewish Feast and Dance. They sat so long over two plates of cakes on the High Table that I did not get any chance to dance, and left after two hours at 6.30 p.m.

I visited Belsen at the end of March and found that Kustermeier was still there, along with 17,000 other displaced persons. I also had a weekend leave in Bad Harzburg, and had an opportunity once again to try ski-ing. There was half a metre of good hard snow, and David J. and I did so well during the first two days that at the end of the second day we ventured on to the slope which had the ski jump and a much steeper angle of descent. This was towards the end of the snow season, and Spring was breaking through with great beauty on the lower slopes.

On my return we learned on the Monday that there was to be another transport to Poland on the Wednesday. Hugh with his staff and I with mine worked till 11 p.m. that night preparing the paper work and making the necessary arrangements. The women in our Team busied themselves with issuing clothing to almost every one of the 700 persons on the list for this transport. All the record cards were ready by mid-day on the Tuesday. Then we received a telephone message : 'Indefinite postponement'. What a great disappointment this was! Bad enough for us to have to put the whole machine in reverse, much worse for the poor Poles themselves, after packing up, disposing of what they could not take with them. My own plans now were to stay another two months, until June at least. Meanwhile I had been exploring the possibilities of articles (apprenticeship) with my solicitor uncle in Wrexham. He had been urging me to read for the Bar, however. Michael was planning to leave in May and work with FRS in London baling clothes until it was time for him to go to University in St. Andrews in September/October. We all had to wait for our discharge dates from the Ministry of Labour & National Service. Mine was not due till September, and I considered going to the Liverpool FRS Friends Service Centre for a while, or working at Friends House London in some capacity.

At the beginning of April we had a power cut lasting several days. As we relied on electricity for cooking our food, this caused the new cooks some difficulties. Two cooks had left recently to prepare for the transport home. This was arranged for the Wednesday, and this time the train was actually coming into the Camp to pick up the people, using the line which connected the aerodrome with the main railway network, which had been idle since the days of the Luftwaffe operations based in the Gypsy Camp aerodrome. The line had now been repaired after bombing. Although in some ways having the train commence its journey in our Camp was convenient, it had the disadvantage that people from all parts of the Brunswick area would be coming in to join the transport, and we had some anxieties about how to manage the operation. Following the departure of so many people, we had to receive more. This involved first cleaning up the vacated accommodation and consolidating the residents so that blocks could be cleared, cleaned and made available. Persuading people to move into different accommodation when they had spent so much effort making themselves comfortable over the winter months involved a great deal of effort on our part. A number of heated and difficult interviews and complicated moves were needed to secure the desired result. Sometimes three or four inter-connected moves were involved in a chain. Then we were in difficulty when one of the parties it was planned to move changed their minds. I commented that 'this kind of work is extremely distasteful to all connected with it. It seems very hard when people have been in the camp the whole winter to force them to move to accommodation which is bound in many cases to be inferior'.

We were now under threat from a fat UNRRA official who was considering coming in and taking over our offices and the whole of Block 1 in order to run an agricultural college for Royalist Yugoslavs! Hugh and Juanita had heard that their services would be required in May in the South of France, and there was some anxiety about his successor. The repatriation was not proceeding as fast as we had hoped, but I felt strongly that a new Team should undertake the fresh and quite different task of dealing with those who were never going to return, as the nature of the work would become entirely different.

We all attended a Folk Song and Dance Festival early in April, which had been organised by the Guides International Service Relief Team. This involved a wonderful programme of individual and collective songs and dances, all in the appropriate national dress, by displaced persons from Estonia, Latvia, Lithuania, the Ukraine, Poland, Yugoslavia, and to cap it all a group of Scottish Highland Dancers. The singing and dancing of the Ukrainian party was particularly fine, and I considered that they would outclass almost any choir from Wales for volume, soundness and clarity in striking the notes and pronouncing the words, and sheer verve and spirit. Their dancing was truly magnificent. Other excellent contributions were made by a couple from Yugoslavia and dancers from that country who did a picturesque trotting dance with minute and delicate steps. The show lasted three hours, and we were all very impressed.

Hugh attended the anniversary of the liberation of Belsen on May 16th. The Jews were laying a commemorative stone on one of the mass graves. I attended various celebrations in Gypsy Camp organised by the ex-concentration camp inmates. The main event in the Camp was the transport to Poland of 688 persons, for which we prepared feverishly for two days. On the Wednesday at 7 a.m. the train ran into the Camp on those disused lines. We had to get our people on board in groups of fifteen, 47 groups in all, in time for the train to leave, which was supposed to be at 11.30 a.m. 300 people from other Camps came to join this train, and different routes had to be signposted for them to reach the train to avoid confusion. One difficulty was to get all the heavy baggage moved to as near the train as possible, using our trucks. Then the railway authorities announced suddenly that the train was due to leave at 9.30 a.m., which caused some panic. However, all the people were aboard by about 10.15 a.m. and the train left at 11 a.m. My storekeeper and one of my office staff left with this transport, as did the Polish Police Chief and our two carpenters, and many other good friends.

Then came the task of emptying block 9 into block 6, and spraying and disinfecting all the rooms. Blocks 2 and 3 were now closed, since we had only 1600 people left. This was the first time since August that the population had dropped below 2,000. Another transport was threatened before Easter, and we knew that many more people would choose to return after Easter. This would ease my mind in choosing this time to leave my work, about the middle of June or thereabouts was what I was planning.

Early in May the Camp received 500 people from Fallingbostel, north of Belsen, where the camps were being closed. A train arrived in the Camp sidings at 8 p.m. in the evening. We had been told at first that there were 1500 on board, of whom 500 should get off and the rest were to proceed another thirty miles to Marienthal. Then we were told there were 800, 400 for us and the remainder to make the extra journey. Actually there were about 537, and we agreed that since it was very late for them to make the extra journey, we should take them all. The arrangements went well, except for the luggage. They had brought so much with them, and all this had to be ferried to the Blocks of residential accommodation. We had only two three-tonners and two ambulances available. All the new arrivals were DDT-dusted and registered at the Theatre under my supervision. It was 1 a.m. before we had finished. Soup, milk for the babies and tea was provided.

The very next day we started work on another Repat transport. There were now a lot of new regulations issued by UNRRA to comply with. We worked till 11 p.m. The next day the train arrived at the Camp, and 259 of our Camp people and about 600 Poles from UNRRA camps and the Guides' Camps joined this train. At 1 p.m. the train left. Unfortunately it did not give a very loud whistle before starting up, and several people who had gone to the camp kitchen to get their soup bowls washed up were left behind. I got my office clerk Janusz to broadcast immediately on the loudspeaker attached to my ambulance, calling all those left behind to come immediately to the ambulance, which I was driving, and about eight very distressed folk arrived in something of a panic. Off I drove and caught up with the train at a level crossing some distance down the road where we lived, Broizemerstrasse. Janusz asked the driver of the train to stop, again using the loudspeaker, and the thankful people rejoined their companions on the train! As the train moved off we saw some silly idiot running along the top of the wagons, jumping from one to the next, so great was the excitement about this moment of repatriation!

Yet another Repat train was arranged early in May. Most of those who left came from the Siegfried Kaserne in north Brunswick, which had to be evacuated to receive 1600 Baltic displaced persons. Many people there felt that, rather than come into another camp, they would prefer to go home, so quite a large proportion of the residents there left on this train. But we could muster only 21 from Gypsy Camp. We still had to undertake the responsibility for all the preparatory work, and a heavy share of the task of marshalling the people as they arrived in lorries and loading the train. Bill R.'s labour gang cleaned up the railway track, which approached our Camp through the ruins of hangars and ground littered with the wreckage of devastated aeroplanes and cars. This enabled the train to run right into the Camp for the first time, but whether this made it easier from the point of view of marshalling and loading was debatable!

There was a sudden rise in the number of people anxious to find employment. Perhaps they were beginning to think they might stay in Germany after all. They were mostly from among the new arrivals from Fallingbostel, and I had a list of forty applicants. We expected some benefit from the new member of our Team who had been a factory welfare officer, and who was now going to take responsibility for Employment and Welfare. A workroom had been started with help from a Red Cross lady, making most attractive dolls, belts and toys out of scrap and salvaged materials. We hoped the scheme would become self-supporting by selling the products in an Army Welfare Shop in the town. We now had two full-time gardeners, who were cleaning and preparing some ground with a view to sowing seed. We also had the seed! I did a bit of gardening myself, digging and clearing round the flats where we lived. One Block had cleared and planted the ground in front of their Block and painted the border railings too.

Suddenly we received notification to expect 200 people from the Siegfried Kaserne the following day. We had enough room, but insufficient beds - only fifty beds were available. At the same time we had to fulfil a requirement from UNRRA to ballot all our residents about repatriation. [A copy of the ballot form appears in an Appendix 5].

The departure of Hugh and Juanita was an occasion to be remembered. On the Friday in question some 200-300 people assembled in the Theatre, together with our Team members. Warm tributes were paid by the new Polish Commandant, the Polish liaison officer who had been with us right through since Belsen, the Polish Delegate from Helmstedt. They mentioned in particular the great support Hugh had always given in official quarters and in countless other ways to the Polish residents in our camp, and the way he had helped in official circles to correct the impression that all Polish displaced persons were bad. They had always denied that they were responsible in any way for the excesses of the handful of racketeers and bandits. Then followed a procession of presentations from the different groups in the Camp; the Nursery School, the School itself, the Boys and Girls Club, the Football Team, the Theatre and Entertainments Committee, the Blockleaders, the Office Staff, the Police, the Territorial Army, the Military Guard, all came up to Hugh and Juanita and made brief speeches, presented bouquets, inscribed scrolls, and presents. It really was a most touching ceremony and a very happy send-off. Hugh and Juanita left the Theatre in a car full of flowers, just as if it were a wedding ceremony!

Jane and Bill R. left on leave, and I took them in my ambulance to Hannover. Beryl W. was the new Team Leader and Assembly Centre Director, with David J. to assist as her Deputy. Having not been long members of the Team, they needed all the help and advice they could get to settle in, and I was glad to be able to offer some assistance. David J. was taking over my work as Registration Officer as well as doing the administrative side of the Director's work, leaving Beryl to attend meetings and conferences but relieving her of the administrative details. A Polish Commandant had arrived and it was hoped that he would take a large share of the responsibility for discipline, internal order, etc. The Police and guards would be under him. He was the third to arrive and attempt to undertake this role!

My negotiations with Cambridge came to nought, since although they at first offered me a place, a review in the light of the very heavy demand forced them to withdraw their offer. I was, however, accepted at L.S.E. for the London University LL.M., which pleased me, since two of my teachers in Wales had been on the Law staff there. I was also considering graduate study in the United States but could find no means of financing this. I wrote about how sorry I would be to leave the work in Brunswick. "In many ways it is the most exciting adventurous, vivid life, in the cockpit of Europe, with never a day without its problem, many disappointments; and now, (in May 1946) more than ever before, rewarding work."

On May 25th I was able to circulate to the School and the Boys and Girls Club a copy (in Polish) of the Welsh Children's Annual Goodwill Message to the Children of the World, which was organised by Rev. Gwilym Davies, President of the Welsh United Nations Association and formerly of The League of Nations Union in Cardiff. I wrote to him about this and received a very warm and gracious reply (see Appendix 7).

By 6th June I had sent my baggage off to England via the Military Forwarding Office, and had nearly completed handing over my responsibilities to David. We went to hear the Glasgow Orpheus Choir presenting a very Scottish programme at the neighbouring town of Wolfenbuttel. I had received thirty pairs of cobblers' lasts from C. & J. Clark in England and these were being put to good use in the shoemakers workshop; no longer were we mending shoes it seems but actually making them! The painters were working well. Altogether "the stage is set for my withdrawal from RT/100 after 18 months' association with it".

I have mentioned my disappointment that Cambridge could no longer offer me a place. The YMCA in Wales, based in Cardiff, would have me back more or less on my own terms. FRS headquarters would give me some temporary work for the summer months. 'What next?', I wrote, 'as the elephant said when it tripped over the flea!" All I wanted was to get out of Brunswick before I became too disheartened and depressed by the circumstances which made life's pattern so uncertain and unjust. Clearly I needed a period of rest and recuperation. The uncertainty about my future plans was weighing heavily upon me. To say, as my family did, that some way would open up, did not help when in my own mind so many ways seem to close down at once. However, I reflected that one's life is not all material happenings, and what I had experienced and seen of the sufferings and distress of mankind, and of the plight of people "on the move", enabled me to see my own situation in a more humble light, and count my blessings! I was really looking forward to a spell of what I believe President Hoover had called after the First World War "a period of normalcy".

My departure for home was delayed by a weekend but I was lucky to be offered a lift by air from the neighbouring RAF, with whom we had played hockey occasionally as well as attending a few of their parties! I resolved to spend the extra days visiting the German courts in Brunswick as well as the British Military Courts. I still possess detailed notes of my observations. In the period of waiting for my departure I felt as if I was living like a Prince on his estate, with no work left on my hands, and so many good friends in the Camp, and so many Departments to visit and see the results of my work therein. It gave me great pleasure and satisfaction at this time of leaving. On my departure I received many presents from all manner of people, including a very handsome paper-weight and letter opener made of aircraft scrap by our German foreman in the Camp, Willi. I was very touched by so much generosity and expressions of appreciation.

So ended the most dramatic and arguably the most important period of my life! Within a few months I had applied for a post as Assistant Lecturer in Law at the University College of Hull (which was not then recognised by the University Grants Committee, and which remained a college preparing students for the University of London External Degree). In the Law Department they also prepared students for the Law Society's examinations, including some ex-Servicemen senior to me in age and with superior knowledge of the law or at least more recent acquaintance with it! Much to my surprise I was appointed, at a salary of £350 per annum, which was raised to £450 later that year when the U.G.C. recognition and funding came through. It was here that I first tried my skills as a university teacher and lecturer, and here that I met my wife, who came from Wales, indeed from my own home town of Cardiff to be precise, and who taught History in the adjacent Girls Grammar School, Newland High. I stayed in Hull four happy years before moving to the Law Department of the London School of Economics, where I happily spent the remainder of my academic career. What place could be better! L.S.E. had been the place of my aspirations ever since my teachers in Wales, the professor and senior lecturer, had shown me the kind of work done there, and opened my eyes to true scholarship, both having tasted what L.S.E. had to offer, one as a member of staff, the other as a graduate student. I never regretted the move.

At the end of July 1946 and early in August the Manchester Guardian and The Times published notices from the Camp residents thanking us for our work. The Guardian notice of 26th July 1946 was rather fuller than The Times, and read:-

BRUNSWICK, ASSEMBLY CENTRE 296, "GYPSY" CAMP IN TAD. KOSCIUSKO

On the anniversary of the opening of the Polish Displaced Persons Camp, Kosciusko, in Brunswick, by the Quaker Team F.R.S. 100, we the residents of this camp would like to express our thanks to the former Section Leader and Camp Commandant, Hugh Jenkins, and his team members for their faithful work and the time which they have devoted for the well-being of the camp.

With the utmost esteem and appreciation of their work, we remain forever grateful D.P.s - their friends.

The Times notice of 3rd August 1946 reads more tersely:

THE POLISH D.P.s from the camp Kosciusko, Brunswick, express their THANKS to the former Section Leader and Camp Commandant, Hugh Jenkins, and his Quaker team for their help and friendship during the past year.

The preparations in London and the journey's beginning

WHAT FOLLOWS DRAWS on a contemporary account of the assembly and departure of our relief team, as seen and experienced by myself and written up, for what purpose I cannot now remember - probably for an F.R.S. house magazine.

This journey began in the back of a lorry on the way to Friends House, London, from Millfield, Highgate. Five of us who had been there on a Driving and Mechanics Course had been called to a meeting to discuss the invitation to join a team for relief work in N.W. Europe. It was with considerable excitement that we boarded the van. Our course was set but little did we know what lay ahead. At Friends House we joined a group of some ten other people, few of whom we knew, to hear two officers of the Overseas and Personnel Departments of FRS outline a request which had come from SHAEF through the British Red Cross and COBSRA to the FRS. A relief team of ten plus one medical "specialist" and two welfare "specialists" was to prepare to leave the country within three weeks. Two out of the five of us were "reserves", the rest of us were "in the team". (I have the list of names in a notebook, Ed.). We were to help organize and distribute relief supplies in co-operation with the Civil Affairs Branch of the Army.

Over the lunch hour we were asked to make up our minds, and this presented me with no difficulty, but two of the prospective team stood down and another dropped out, and the three reserves were brought in. One of our five was still a "reserve" but we were glad that the other was now included.

In the afternoon, after accepting the invitation to join the team, we filled in a clothing coupon application, were vaccinated and inoculated against typhoid, para-typhoid and tetanus, and saw the Personnel Department and arranged to finish whatever jobs we had been doing. Then we acquainted ourselves with the other members of the team, and after pooling ideas about what personal equipment was advisable, we parted for a week's embarkation leave, feeling a little staggered by the rapid progress of events.

The Assembly of the Team and The Preparations

When we re-assembled at Mount Waltham a week later, with stories of the hectic time we had clearing up our personal affairs and visiting relations and friends, we had our first real meeting as a team. We sorted out the various tasks to be tackled immediately and shared them out between us. Some were deputed to collect information about Holland, the country we expected to be going to, some to arrange talks and language lessons, some to see to censorship of books (what this means escapes me at the present time!), some to arrange for the selection and supply of tools and stationery.

Most of us had already started keeping lists of the little things suggested to be done and to take with us, and henceforward these lists grew rapidly from day to day, despite constant elimination of items already dealt with. We spent a great deal of the little spare time we had wrestling with these lists. I still have my notebook containing these lists!

I had attended a short course on overseas relief work at Mount Walthamn the previous April, so the set-up was not wholly unfamiliar to me, and I settled down quickly. At this point we were invited to attend one of the meetings of the Overseas Committee of F.R.S. No doubt they were as anxious to meet us as we were curious to met them. We were also briefed about equipment by the Overseas Equipment Officer and the Overseas Secretary gave us a further outline of the kind of work we might be expected to undertake "over there". We were issued with a down sleeping bag, sheet inners, a canvas bucket, and a torch. Various items of clothing were purchased with supplementary clothing coupons, from a wholesale store and from the F.A.U. and other sources.

The R.A.O.C. provided an extensive variety of useful equipment, for the men, for example, underclothing, kitbag, blanket, tin helmet, (which had to be painted grey: see below), gas equipment, two pairs of boots (I still use one pair for heavy gardening), a hair-brush, boot-brushes (still in regular use in 1993), a mess tin and eating utensils. "The 'housewife' in our list turned out to be nothing more than what is sometimes called a hussif or needle and thread, and the 'mug (doubtful)' never materialised at all!"

We were to wear grey uniforms because the Friends Relief Service of which we were members had refused to wear khaki uniforms in case we were identified with the military. This was part of our pacifist stand, and had led to some delays in getting permission from SHAEF (Supreme Headquarters Allied Expeditionary Force) to enter the field of combat otherwise than in khaki uniform. (The Friends Ambulance Unit wore khaki but their work was primarily as medical auxiliaries although in the end they did a lot of useful social and relief work, especially in Greece.) The grey uniforms fitted poorly especially for the women and were made of rather coarse material which proved hot and uncomfortable in the summer. We were later to be mistaken for German troops on a number of occasions in Germany.

The uniforms had been made for us by the Co-op, but we collected various items of Army issue from a Depot in South London before our departure, including two pairs of Army boots, together with 'puttees' which were khaki and which we painstakingly dyed grey, boot-brushes and satchels, water-bottles and the like. We carefully stamped each item with our initials. The rather ill-fitting uniforms consisted of a jacket and skirt for the women and a blouson and trousers for the men, bearing shoulder flashes with the words 'Quaker Relief', with grey berets. We also had received some rather thick grey shirts, and some army underwear, including long johns.

Turning the khaki equipment into grey involved a tedious process. First the equipment was dye-ed black, and then blanco-ed RAF blue, a process which often had to be repeated to obtain a satisfactory result. Moreover each item of equipment had to be stencilled clearly with one's name and "Friends Relief Service (Quakers)" or "F.R.S.". Wooden items had to be stamped with a metal die and metal surfaces scratched with the initials. Clothing had to be marked with ink or name-tapes had to be sewn in, and shoulder tabs had to be sewn on our uniforms. Here a healthy division of labour sprang into being, the women members of the team doing the sewing while the men did the heavier work. Weighing and packing all this equipment completed the process of preparation. I managed to make an extra two grey ties from gym slip girdle material which was coupon-free, cut into suitable lengths. Wearing the uniform in public for the first time was a trying experience, in more senses than one, especially for those for whom extensive alterations had proved necessary for decency and comeliness, it seems. On one of our first trips out so attired, we were rather self-conscious, but the uniforms seem to have met with approving glances and interested attention from some children and members of the public.

Towards the time appointed for our departure it became clear that this would be delayed, and we were mildly thankful about that. Several members of the Team were still awaiting their release from essential work, and our equipment was by no means complete.

All this physical activity was interspersed with briefing by people who were familiar with our destination or with conditions of life in a recently liberated territory, with language lessons from two separate teachers, driving tests, dental appointments, and further inoculations against diphtheria, typhus, and a further dose of the dreaded TABT (typhoid, paratyphoid and tetanus injection) which laid some of our team members low the first time.

From week to week new departure dates were mooted only to be unrealised and further postponements endured. Our tasks were re-organised, the welfare "specialists" being merged in with the rest of the team, now re-inforced by the joining of a new member, and we had to get used to these changes. We ourselves allotted among the team members the various tasks which COBSRA had suggested should be designated. These were Leader, Quartermaster, Nurse, Assistant Nurse, Clerk, Accountant, Registration Officer, Sanitation and Hygiene Officer, Cook-Caterer, Information Officer, Welfare Officer, Driver/mechanic, and two Drivers. The three women who had social work experience were asked to nominate one of their members to be 'assistant nurse'. The role fell to Joyce P. since she had done a first aid course!

The typhus injections were done at Burroughs & Wellcome's laboratories in Euston Road. At this time I remember how I sought to procure a cane frame for the large canvas rucksack which I had bought to carry my personal belongings. Having tried the Institute for the Blind, some kind person directed me to a workshop in an alley off Charing Cross Road. There I was able to have a cane frame made up to order for a modest outlay, and this served the purpose well enough until the rucksack was eventually retired. The preparations continued apace, there were busy days spent collecting and marking our equipment. A break for Christmas was very welcome, and we returned refreshed to tackle the final preparations. Dutch lessons and orientation lectures continued, and at one point during the hiatus of waiting for embarkation orders members of the team were sent off on different temporary assignments. I was sent with two other members to the clothing store at Witley, Surrey, while other members of the Team went elsewhere.

Some went to the children's hostel at Brinkley to meet a crisis which had arisen due to illness among the staff. Some went for experience to the F.R.S. Quartermaster's Office at the London Hospital Students' Hostel at Aldgate East. Some went to Haddo to help in F.R.S. workshops. Extra driving tuition was arranged for two members, two worked with COBSRA for a while, Joyce P. acquired some nursing experience by working in the Out-Patient Department at the Hackney Hospital. Several members were shown the workings of the Searcher Service for Refugees, etc. at Bloomsbury House, and visited the workshops of the Nursery Schools Association.

The work at Witley involved sorting and packing clothing to be sent to Greece. There was some kind of emergency about it, and three of our Team who were free to go went there for a while to help (Jane L., Beth C. and me). There, inside a huge pavilion situated in the woods we found shelf after shelf containing hundreds of items of clothing, some in boxes, some in bales, some loosely piled up. Our task was to pack the clothing in bales which were tightly pressed in a baling machine and roped up. Then they were stencilled in large letters and addressed to the Greek Red Cross. We slept on the job in rather primitive conditions, with only a blanket separating the men and the women, bales one side, boxes at our feet, and above our heads shelves of sacks, destined for France. A stack of soap at the far end of the pavilion was held in reserve. The soap and shoes for Greece had already been packed. Also overcoats, coats, men's clothing, women's clothes, clothes for boys and girls and for babies, bandages and packs or pochettes containing face flannel, soap, toothpaste and brush, as well as sewing aids. There were also some tools. The shipment for Greece had been given the all-clear by General Alexander, and it was hoped they would catch the next boat. This was the emergency for which our help had been needed. By every post we were receiving parcels and bundles of clothing, for example, 35 pochettes from the County School, Lincoln, mixed clothing from the Presbyterian Church at Walthamstow, a little parcel from Menai Bridge in North Wales. Suddenly the railway delivered nineteen more sacks of clothes and there was chaos everywhere.

After Christmas, we had moved to fresh quarters in the Bedford Institute, Quaker Street, in the East End close to Liverpool Street Station and Petticoat Lane. We collected more equipment from the RAOC. "The vests are warm, the pants like hessian". A talk from Roger Wilson one night after supper at the Bedford Institute discussed such vital topics as 'should one drink wine in a tea-garden or with officers in a mess when wearing Quaker uniform?'. I spent some days helping COBSRA (the Council of British Societies for Relief Abroad) with a delivery of several tons of clothing destined for the Jewish Committee for Relief Abroad, which had to be carried to the top floor of their offices, and with some menial office work of a clerical nature. I also collected thirty drivers' oilskins and trousers from an RAOC depot at Streatham Ice Rink. Later it was discovered that the Major at the headquarters of the Deputy Ordnance Officer Commanding in Leconfield

House, Curzon Street had omitted to indent for goggles, so I had to return all the way there to obtain a fresh indent and go back again to Streatham, this time by tram! It took a long time.

On Tuesday, January 30th 1945 the Team extended a welcome to parents, spouses and friends and F.R.S. officers at a Farewell Reception at the Friends International Centre, Gordon Square. This was in the afternoon and took the form of a talk which was supposed to be followed by a film showing our Team preparations. The film show failed to materialise, as the machine broke down! There is a story to be told about this, as I was in charge of the projector, but I would prefer to draw a veil over this!

On January 31st we had attended a tea reception at the Y.W.C.A. as an informal opening of a two-day COBSRA course. Here for the first time we met the other members of the North West Europe "Spearhead" Civilian Relief Unit, which we were told should number 182 persons in all. There was a most impressive array of khaki uniforms bedecked with all manner of badges of rank, flashes, tapes and ribbons - worn by all manner of bodies, from lah-di-dah women and flashy girls who wanted "to do their little bit" - to a retired Army officer complete with monocle. Our Quaker grey uniforms and the navy-blue of the Salvation Army provided a little variety; the former provoked curious enquiry, while the latter is of course well-known.

The course itself proved very helpful, giving us a much clearer idea of the work we might be expected to do, and the way in which it might be tackled. The most encouraging feature was the spirit in which the leaders urged us to tackle the work, including Mr. H. from COBSRA, Brigadier S. (British Red Cross Commission) and others. Lady Falmouth of the British Red Cross Commission in particular mentioned at the Team Reception that no differences of feeling about war and peace should prevent us from doing the job which we were setting out to do, which was a humanitarian venture of the highest order. On a later occasion she urged us not to withhold relief from the German people, as we could not honestly discriminate. Where there were needs to be met, they should be met without discrimination.

We still-had to collect our vehicles, and this was now arranged. On 9th and 10th February three of us went to Shrewsbury with one F.A.U. member to collect our two ambulances, together with fourteen others. We stayed the night at the YMCA and YWCA and were very well treated, having our first experience of an Army canteen, and getting the food and drink at privileged prices, it seems. This obviously made quite an impression.

Two others went off to Derbyshire to collect the 3-tonner, which turned out to be a 5-ton Leyland, which was eventually exchanged for an Austin 3-

tonner with six wheels. The whole of this convoy experienced some difficulty getting back to London as the vehicles were in a very poor state, having been left in the open unattended for some time. Later the two small Bedford 15-cwt trucks were collected, and the unit was complete so far as transport was concerned. At first we parked in Mount Waltham, but after an inspection in Belgrave Square in the week of 14th February we decided to keep the vehicles loaded and parked under guard in Quaker Street outside the Bedford Institute. This was the time when Michael and I went on a little trip to Wembley one Sunday afternoon to collect certain items of equipment (134 hurricane lamps) which were missing from the comprehensive issue received from the Quartermasters' Department.

The waiting continued for weeks which became months. Dr. Louis F. was informed he could not get his release after all, the Ministry of Labour withdrew it, which was a bitter disappointment to us all, and "put him in a fine soup", it seems. By this time we were on 6 hours call to leave.

Still no news of our departure was forthcoming, however, and we grew impatient. "The rush to get packed was followed by the deepest despair when nothing happened." The weekend passed, a new week began and we went off for a few days' leave. I went with Michael to his home in Sussex, and as we arrived there the phone rang and we were told to re-assemble on the morrow. There followed hectic packing and a hurried departure from Quaker Street.

Having cleared everything from the Bedford Institute premises and packed our vehicles, we drove to one of the large London parks, spending the night at Gordon House, Highgate, one of the F.R.S. hostels, rather grandly described as an Overseas Assembly Centre. The next day we started off early and assembled our convoy in Belgrave Square, one of the large London squares where the headquarters of the British Red Cross was situated. Here we sat a whole day, by turn getting hot and cold, and without access to toilets so we used the park! At one point we were besieged by several press photographers and journalists, as well as an inspection by V.I.P.s

At last we moved off, driving slowly under police escort, through the City of London and the East End to camp the night outside Tilbury docks. We had instructions not to let any other vehicle come between the vehicles of the convoy and to ignore all red traffic lights. My letter records with some delight how I had driven across four red lights! My wife says I have been doing it ever since!! We spent the night parked by the roadside, the drivers stayed with their vehicles, sleeping in a tented transit camp, the others in a hostel. Was this the time when I fed in an Army Officers' Mess for the first time? The tented accommodation by the roadside included the services of a batman who roused us and brought early morning tea. I made a last minute phone call home the previous night, without being able to reveal our whereabouts. When we drove down to the dockside, the sight of our ship excited us - but, alas, we were to be disappointed - there was something wrong with it and we had to wait for the next one to come in.

The voyage was a long one, it was a rather stormy night, and many of the party (including myself) were sick. It was a Tank Landing Craft which had a rather shallow draft and bobbed about in the sea a lot, as well as belching diesel fumes. We arrived in Ostend in the early hours, glad to reach dry land.

APPENDIX 2

RUDOLF KUSTERMEIER - a German ex-concentration camp inmate who had been imprisoned in Berlin in 1933, and subsequently moved to Belsen. An account of my meetings with him there and afterwards, and the correspondence with Corder Catchpool.

ON MAY 2ND 1945, while I was ferrying the patients from the Human Laundry at Belsen to the hospital blocks, Major G. the R.A.M.C. officer in charge of the place asked me to look up Rudolf Kustermeier, a German who came out of the Concentration Camp bearing a letter E on his forehead written in iodine; this was to signify that he could speak English and might therefore be of some use as an interpreter. I found him acting in this capacity in the Men's Ward. He was delighted to meet me, and came to supper that night. It was then that he told me that one reason for the starvation in Camp 1 had been that the bakery at Celle, the neighbouring town, had been bombed three times, and this had been the source of their bread supply. Thereafter it had to be brought all the way from Hamburg but was bombed on the way. Of course this only partly accounted for the food shortages in Camp 1.

His own story was that as a socialist journalist working in Berlin before the War he had been sentenced to ten years' imprisonment in 1933 which time he spent in different prisons. Upon his release in 1943 he was sent to a Concentration camp, latterly in Belsen, where he had developed a stomach ulcer and was rather weak and debilitated. In Berlin he had known the Quaker Corder Catchpool, who was working there in the thirties, and asked me if he could be put in touch with him. He was now living in Hampstead. He was also anxious to find his wife, Elisabeth, last known to be in Berlin. I wrote to Friends House, London, to ask them to make inquiries about Corder Catchpool, and in due course received a letter from him saying how delighted he was to be remembered by Rudi Kustermeier and asking me to forward a letter to him.

Meanwhile I was in frequent contact with Rudi, and we became good friends. For example, my diary records that on May 4th we talked about the interviews he had had with Field Security, about the reasons for the lack of anti-Nazi underground movements in Germany, and about Friends' work since the war. "Jane came in and told us the war in N.W. Europe is over as from tomorrow 8 a.m." My diary does not record our response, but we were no doubt overjoyed.

The following Sunday he attended our Meeting for Worship, and I recorded that it was very impressive to have his company, and I loaned him some literature. On May 11th Kustermeier came to visit us in our new quarters. On May 14th I went to collect him and arranged with Ted B. that he should receive some more clothing and later I learned that he received everything except a jacket. I later visited him in his room. On May 18th Kustermeier was trying to see me all day but without success, I was too busy. I saw him the next day, however, and we had a long talk about his personal problems, about socialism and the future of Germany. I discovered that he had details of all the German anti-Fascists in the Camp. The next day he attended our Meeting for Worship.

In the third week in May, after the burning of the huts and the final clearing of Camp 1, we moved to Sulingen. I saw Rudi before we left, and was able to show him Corder Catchpool's letter. He was very touched, particularly that Corder had referred to him as "Rudi" which only his most intimate friends at that time called him. He also said that the most wonderful thing which happened to him in Bergen-Belsen was to meet us there. He never thought when the British troops arrived that some Quakers would be along as well! I gave him some clothing and toilet requisites as well as some newspapers. It was arranged that he would visit the burgermeister at the nearby village of Bergen. [There is another amazing coincidence which Joyce recalls. While we were at Sulingen she met a German who was in the British Army Pioneer Corps. When she told him how we had recently been in Belsen Camp, he asked if by any chance we had any news of Rudi Kustermeier, whom he had known in pre-war Berlin all those years ago. Joyce was happy to give him the news that Rudi had survived all those years in prison and the concentration camps, and of our encounter with him in Belsen.]

The next day, May 25th, Rudi turned up again. He had spent one hour searching everywhere for a little gift for us. We told him we would not forget Belsen in a hurry but that it was very charming of him and much appreciated.

During the time we were at Sulingen it did not prove possible for me to visit Belsen and renew our contact, but as soon as we reached Brunswick and had settled in, I took the first opportunity to go to Belsen in order to find out how he was getting on. This was on June 15th. There was a letter awaiting me from him, and I managed to find him. He was now sharing a room with a Latvian lady who eventually became his wife, after he discovered that his first wife Elizabeth had divorced him under a law of Nazi Germany which permitted this to be done in respect of political prisoners. The lady in question had been in the Camps with him and it seemed right that Rudi should make a fresh start in this way, and I was glad that he had some-one to care for him, for his health was by no means good.

I wrote to Corder Catchpool informing him of my visit. My diary contains no further references to my encounters with Rudi, but in my letters home there are frequent references.

The first letter from Corder Catchpool was acknowledged by Rudolf Kustermeier in a long reply, dated June 1st, 1945. He writes from Square 6, Canteen 6, Hospital Area, Belsen camp, saying that he is unable to express his happiness when he read 'your kind lines, and thus to see renewed a connection which through many years has meant so much to me. As I am now allowed to write everywhere I wish to express to you my many thanks by this first letter I send to England after our liberation by the British Army'.

He recalls a visit which Catchpool made to Brandenburg Prison in June or July 1936 when he had tried to see their mutual friend Rene Batholet. Rudi had wished to see the visitor too on that occasion, but knew that there was no possibility of getting permission. He goes on to give a detailed account of his time in prison since 1933.

"At first I was at Luckau and then at Brandenburg prison. Two years of solitary confinement was a rather good time for me. My labour was not too hard and I never felt so lonely as many of my comrades did because I lived with many good authors (sic. books Ed.) by whom I learnt more and with whom I had more profitable discussions than I ever could have done with my fellow-sufferers. For more than one year I had to make paper-bags, another year I produced play-things for the children. Then I worked as a book-binder, afterwards as a librarian and so on. In September 1940 I was transferred to Sonnenburg (near the River Oder). There I had my best time. The labour was very hard; we had to cut trees for a paper mill. For a long time I was unable to accomplish what was fixed as a normal amount for us. But as our guards with whom we were along in the wide forests without seeing anybody else, were really good men, and as we had food enough (we got many extras by (sic. from Ed.) the owner of the woods), I gradually became stronger so that afterwards I enjoyed very much my always being in the open air, even in winter time when it was terribly cold and the snow reaching up to our knees. In January 1943 I came back to Brandenburg because long-time prisoners (8 years or more) were no longer allowed to work outside the walls. I got a job in the administration of the prison (book-keeping and revision) and at last worked as a secretary to kitchen-staff. So I could do good and useful work, and, on the whole, I was not too much discontented with my situation."

"Things changed terribly when, in January 1944, the 10 years of my Volksgerichtshef sentence were over. Now the Gestapo sent me to Grossbeeren Camp near Berlin. Here I saw for the first time all the terrible excesses of the SS guards which now have become known everywhere. A few days after my arrival, the camp was set under quarantine because we had typhus. There was no hospital in the camp and no treatment at all. I heard afterwards that two-thirds of the whole camp had died. I myself and a few other Germans and Dutchmen were transferred to a Berlin Hospital. We were regarded and treated as "Aryans" while the Polish and Russian men who composed nine-tenths of the camps were allowed to die where they were, lying on the floors with their shirt and two blankets only."

"In the Hospital, Elisabeth was allowed to send me parcels and later even to see me. Unfortunately shortly after I overcame my fever I was infected with Diphtheria by a Dutch patient coming into my room as a typhus case. His having Diphtheria at the same time had not been recognised. I got through for the second time but I was so weak that I could not walk for months. At that time Elisabeth succeeded in arguing that I was quite unable to do anything dangerous to the Nazi-Government and she was allowed to take me home for the time of my recovery. In December 1944 I was arrested once more and now brought to Sachsenhausen Cranienburg Camp. I was not yet able to work and fortunately I was not forced to. Many of the workshops of the camp had not enough raw materials or machines, so there were more workers than they could employ. When, in the first days of February, the Russians approached the Oder, the camp was partially evacuated to other places in different parts of Germany. So I came to Belsen Camp which will have been one of the most horrible places the world has ever seen. Perhaps you will know that 16,000 of us have died from April 1st to 15th. When the British troops came we were 39,500 men, women and children alive. None of us will ever forget what we have gone through and perhaps you will understand our situation as it was when I say that many of us now cannot believe that we really have seen the things we remember. They are too terrible to be imagined or described, there are no words for it."

The letter describes his uncertainty about the future. He was still awaiting news of his wife Elisabeth, and about his mother and sisters he still had no news. He says that the Friends Relief Team had helped him so much to find his way back - no, forward, to normal life once again.

He ends this long letter by remarking that he does not yet know what the future will bring for him. He says that he considers that "... I should be allowed to be confident after my having been saved from the greatest horrors ever to be imagined".

The rest of the story may be told quite briefly. With some assistance from the military authorities he left Belsen for Hamburg in search of employment as a journalist. He got good introductions, and I was glad to be able to give him some money for the journey (£8 as I remember). He ended up as Hauptschriftsleiter (Editor) of Die Welt, Hamburg, a national newspaper which was inaugurated by the British Control Commission. On its being handed over to German management he became Foreign Correspondent, and in this capacity visited Britain in 1947, and reported on the situation there as he observed it. News cuttings show his concern for the plight of German prisoners-of-war still held in camps in Britain. Later on, in 1950, he returned to report the British General Election. I met him at this time and remember his vivid description of how he had attended an election meeting in the mining valleys of South Wales at Ebbw Vale, which the sitting Member of Parliament for that constituency Aneurin Bevan was due to address. He was deeply impressed by the way the audience all joined in singing hymns while they waited for the great man to arrive.

In 1962 my wife and I spent a month in Israel while I was taking part in an International Course on Criminology at the Hebrew University of Jerusalem. We arranged to meet Rudi Kustermeier (and his second wife Fanny), who by this time was Israeli Correspondent for the German Press Agency Deutsche Presse Agence. One afternoon he took us on a Sabbath to the museum of the holocaust at Yad Veshem, and we drove through some villages where orthodox Jews resided, and I remember vividly how we endured the jeers and stone throwing of the young kids in the street. He told me then of the trial of Eichmann and how he had been the sole civilian allowed to attend the execution of Eichmann, being given this 'privilege' on account of his background. He was absolutely opposed to capital punishment even for such a man as that.

We exchanged letters afterwards, and I learned how he was undecided whether to stay in Israel or go back to Germany. Sonja his daughter was learning English and very happy in school, and eventually they moved into a nice new flat and seemed very comfortable. His health continued to cause problems, but otherwise he seemed content. We lost touch after that, but I think it important to preserve the memory of our brief contacts, and to record the suffering that many decent Germans endured under the Nazi authorities, side by side with the displaced persons from so many different countries and the Jews from everywhere.

Belsen Memorial Gardens, September 1988

APPENDIX 3

NOTES ON BELSEN CAMP, issued by Colonel H.W. Bird, Commander, 102 Control Section, Second Army (issued the day of the burning ceremony)

1. We feel that some of you who were not here at BELSEN from the beginning might like to see these notes. They give the most accurate facts available. We would like to have produced them before, but we were one and all rather busy on the first main job of clearing the Concentration Camp.
   That job is now finished.

2. On 12th April, 1945, the Chief of Staff of the first German Para Army approached the Brigadier General Staff of the British Eighth Corps. He said that a terrible situation had arisen at Belsen, and that Typhus was raging there. He asked us to come in and take the place over.

   On 13th April, 1945, the Terms of a special Truce were drawn up. (You must remember that a battle was going on all around the Belsen area.) Under these terms the British agreed to come in and take over the Camp; a neutral area was defined around Belsen; the S.S. Camp Staff were to remain, the British doing what they liked with them; and the Hungarians to remain, armed, and be used by the British until such time as they had no further use for them.

   It is believed that Brigadier Glyn Hughes, Deputy Director of Medical Services, Second Army, was the first to arrive.

   The first British Unit in was an anti-Tank Battery of 63 Anti-Tank Regt. They arrived on 15th April, 1945. Lieut.Col. Johnston, with 32 CCS, came in on 17th April, 1945. Lieut.Col. Mather with 113 Light AntiAircraft Regt, Headquarters 10 Garrison, and 224 Military Government Detachment (Major Miles) came in on 18th April, 1945, when 113 LAA took over from the Anti-Tank Battery.

The scene which met the first comers beggars description. There were approximately 50,000 people in the Camp, of which about 10,000 lay dead in the huts or about the Camp. Those still alive had had no food or water for about seven days, after a long period of semi-starvation. Typhus, amongst other diseases, was raging. Corruption and filth was everywhere, the very air was poisoned. You have no doubt heard these terrible details from those who saw them.

The tasks which faced the first comers must have appeared insurmountable. Nevertheless, they were tackled with amazing success, when one considers the resources available.

With the arrival of the first BRCS teams, and Col. Spottiswoode of Military Government, on 21st April, 1945, the first of the flow of reinforcements began - which went on until we are the large party you know now. On 30th April, 1945, 102 Control Section, Second Army, took over command and control of the Camps and installations from Headquarters 10 Garrison.

3. The first big job is now over.
On 19th May, 1945, the Concentration Camp will have been cleared of the last person. All its inmates will then have been moved to the four hospitals and the three Transit Camps in the Barracks' Area.
A total of 28,900 will have been evacuated from that Camp, of whom 2,006 have died since coming out.
The British have supervised the burial by SS and German PW of some 23,000 of which approximately 10,000 or even more lay unburied when they arrived here on 15th April, 1945.
The daily death rate has been terribly high, but is steadily decreasing. On 30th April, 1945, 548 people died. 97 died on 17th May, 1945.

4. You have no doubt noticed the miraculous change that takes place in the inmates of the Camp when they have been up here in Hospitals or Transit Camps for a few days.

500 fit started their homeward journey to western Europe on 17th May, 1945.

Another 7,000 will be leaving, mostly for countries in Eastern Europe, between 22-23rd May, 1945.

This place will then consist of four Hospitals containing about 13,000 people, and two transit camps (III and IV) with about 6,400.

They will all eventually leave here as they become fit to travel.

5. We are now burning down the Concentration Camp, and intended holding the Ceremony of burning the lst hut on 21st May, 1945, at six o'clock in the evening.

That should end the First Chapter in the history of Belsen since the British came.

The next and final chapter will be the nursing back to health in the hospitals of the thousands who are sick in mind and body.

Headquarters,	H.W. Bird,
BELSEN Camp,	Colonel,
18th May, 1945	Commander 102 Control Section,
HLWB/EFP	SECOND Army.

APPENDIX 4

COPY OF LETTER from Col. Agnew, Deputy Commissioner, B.R.C. Commission (Civilian Relief), thanking the relief teams for their work in Belsen : 19th June 1945.

> HQ 5.
> British Red Cross Commission
> (Civilian Relief),
> B.L.A.
>
> 19th June 1945

To: Relief Sections   100 - 103 - 104
                        105 - 113 - 114

The following has been received from General Lindsay, Commissioner of British Red Cross for N.W. Europe:

"I have had letters from both Lady Limerick and Lady Falmouth which are full of appreciation of the work being done by your teams. Both emphasize the splendid liaison which those teams are getting with their opposite numbers in Holland.

"As regards the Teams in Belsen, Lady Falmouth says as follows:-

'I wanted to tell you how enormously impressed I was with the work of our teams at Belsen - in all that atmosphere of horror and ghastliness - still all-pervading even though the actual horrors had gone - it really did warm my heart and make me terribly proud that the English, and in particular our own Red Cross and Voluntary Society teams, had given such devoted service, and had worked such a wonderful transformation in those poor souls as we saw everywhere. If not one other piece of Civilian Relief had ever been done or was done in the future, they have already made the work worth-while; they have added a very glorious page to the history of the British Red Cross and the

Friends War Relief Service. If it is not too much trouble, could you convey this to the teams and the Doctors who have done so much.

'It was very cheering to hear the most unstinted and glowing praise from all the Army at the Camp. They certainly appreciate all that our teams have done. I was delighted too with the general appearance of the team workers. They still looked fit and hard and cheerful, and not a bit "got down" by their experiences - they should be very seasoned troops by now!'

'I think you will agree that no praise could be higher. Will you please convey this to the leaders of all your teams, and add that I, myself, am so delighted that the splendid work they are all doing has been so much appreciated by our visitors from headquarters in London.'

"Well done all! I hope to be seeing you all again in the near future.

K.M. Agnew,
Deputy Commissioner,
B.R.C. Commission,
(Civilian Relief)."

APPENDIX 5

QUESTIONNAIRE FORM 1 (printed in Polish and German as well as English)

UNRRA

INDIVIDUAL QUESTIONNAIRE ON REPATRIATION

Below are three questions which every Displaced Person in Germany is being asked to answer. You will note that your name is not asked for and that this questionnaire is a secret ballot.

1. What is your nationality? ....

2. Do you wish to be repatriated? ....
$$\qquad\qquad\qquad\qquad\qquad\qquad\text{(Yes or No)}$$

3. If your answer to question 2 is "NO", explain your reasons in the space below:

May 1946

APPENDIX 6

LETTER TO GEORGE M.LL. DAVIES, a prominent Welsh peace worker, 8.11.45, subsequently published in the Welsh weekly newspaper 'Y Faner' - about conditions in Berlin [English translation]

8.11.45

Dear George Davies,

Here is a short account of my activities since my return from leave to my work at Brunswick.

Yesterday I had the great privilege of meeting Hans Albrecht, the Clerk of Yearly Meeting of the Society of Friends [Quakers] in Germany, who paid us a visit.

He had travelled from Berlin on one of the trucks involved in 'Operation Stork' which is bringing a number of children from the German capital to spend the winter in The British Zone. I went to a village on the border of The Russian Zone to collect him and his secretary, so I was able to see the Camp where the children are spending the night on the journey to the West. The children appear to be in fairly good health but it should be remembered that each child has a detailed medical examination before being accepted, so that the weak and the sick are not allowed to come. Also each child has to bring blankets and a supply of clothes, and no doubt some are prevented from coming for this reason. I understand that all the arrangements for moving the children are working extremely smoothly, and no doubt we shall see before the Spring the advantages of this arrangement, and we should be grateful to those who have enabled it to come about. More movements like this are sorely needed, and more of the imagination which lies behind them.

A quiet and gentle person over sixty years of age, very Germanic in appearance, Hans has the habit of thrusting his round head forward towards one as he speaks, and he sounds very grave.

And it is a grave story which he has to tell. He inquired first about our time in Antwerp, Belsen, Sulingen and Brunswick. Then he described conditions in Berlin, and in particular the behaviour of the Russian troops there. He confirmed the stories about rape, pillage and destruction which had occurred in the first days of liberation, and said this was still going on in the nearby suburbs. Almost all the young women had been raped, and that was every night. Those who resisted or were found hiding were shot. Sometimes these unwelcome visitors came as often as eight times in one night to the same home.

At the present time there are grave food shortages, specially in the countryside, where the situation was made worse by the habit of the Russians stealing all the supplies the farmers had, in order to provide for some suburb or town, and all this in an unplanned manner or contrary to orders. In the capital itself things had improved somewhat, with a new rationing system which was working reasonably well. However women were not getting their fair share of rations, since according to normal Russian practice, they had been placed in the fifth class in terms of priority. This means they get what is left over after others have been supplied. There was no coal, and electricity and gas were severely rationed.

It is very quiet in Berlin these days. One can walk for miles in almost any direction only to find empty streets in ruins, bare walls and chimneys, and the damp smell of decay to remind one of the life that was there before.

Industrial production was quickly restored, a large number of cinemas are open and the occasional theatre. There is only half the traffic there used to be, buses, trams and underground trains are few, and out of 300 trains which used to run from one suburb before the war there were only eighty at the present time.

What about the prospects? The birth-rate is down, the death rate up, in one district it had reached seven times the birth-rate. It is thought there will be twelve million refugees under the new arrangements, and that four or five million people will die. It is estimated that one hundred per cent of children under the age of one year will die before the Spring, and fifty per cent of the children aged between one year and three years. In addition to those refugees there are the German ex-servicemen returning from Russia in a worse plight if that is possible from having been prisoners of war. Only the sick and injured are allowed to return, and they arrive in Berlin in very poor shape.

After painting this grim picture, Hans told us what weighed on his mind daily in experiencing all this misery, and what his convictions were. Firstly, he thought that the British and the Americans could do more to alleviate all this suffering. Secondly, he could not for the life of him understand how the British and Americans could put up with all that was happening, when they had just fought a war with all their might against cruelty, slavery and the like.

Some marvellous things had been done by the authorities, such, as with careful, detailed and enlightened planning, swiftly arranging for the evacuation of 50,000 children from Berlin before the winter arrives. But only the children aged between 3 and 14 were being moved and not all of them. What about the remainder? This did show what can be done.

It was a great pleasure for this brave Quaker to be among those who shared his views. He believed we were all members of the same human family, but regretted that some had not realised the dire plight of others.

Sincerely yours,
    Eryl

APPENDIX 7

THE WELSH CHILDREN'S PEACE MESSAGE, May 1946 and Letter from Rev. Gwilym Davies, President, Welsh National Council, United Nations Association.

Distribution to School, Boys' Club, Girls' Club, Nursery School

Welsh Children's Message to the Children of the World 18.5.46

I enclose a Polish version of the Annual Message which has been sent out from Wales every year since 1922 in the name of the Children of Wales to the Children of the World. Before the War, the Message grew slowly to cover the whole world, and replies were received from 60 countries. A special radio programme was arranged not only from the BBC in Wales but also in Paris, Geneva, Warsaw, Copenhagen, Prague, Stockholm, in some of the United States radio stations, in S. America and the Dominions. The 18th of May, "Goodwill Day", is very widely observed, and now once more the message comes this year to us in our Camp in Brunswick. The Welsh people have not forgotten the Displaced Persons, and we have received many parcels of clothing and soap, pencils and schoolbooks from the Welsh children. Perhaps you will bring this letter to the attention of the young people of the Camp.

EHW

113

Twenty-fifth Annual Message from the Children of Wales to the Children of the World
18th May 1946

BOYS AND GIRLS OF ALL NATIONS! WE, THE BOYS AND GIRLS OF WALES GREET YOU ONCE MORE. TODAY IS GOODWILL DAY. YOUTH HAILS YOUTH ACROSS LAND AND SEA, IN THE NAME OF FREEDOM AND FRIENDSHIP.

WE REJOICE THAT PEACE HAS COME AND THAT ALL THE PEOPLES ARE MAKING A NEW EFFORT TO END ALL WARS.

WE DESIRE A WORLD WHERE NEVER AGAIN SHALL MILLIONS OF HOMES BE DESTROYED, WHERE NEVER AGAIN SHALL COUNTLESS LITTLE CHILDREN DIE OF STARVATION.

WE DESIRE A WORLD WHERE NEVER AGAIN SHALL ONE NATION LIVE IN FEAR OF ANY OTHER NATION.

WE DESIRE A WORLD WHERE THE NATIONS SHALL CO-OPERATE ONE WITH THE OTHER FOR THE COMMON GOOD, TRUSTING EACH OTHER AT ALL TIMES AND SHARING TOGETHER ALL THE WEALTH AND RICHES OF THE EARTH.

THROUGH OUR DARING AND COURAGE, THROUGH OUR THOUGHTS AND DEEDS, WE CAN ASSIST TO BRING THIS NEW SPIRIT TO THE WORLD, AND THIS WE WILL DO!

YOUNG PEOPLE OF THE WORLD! LET US DEVOTE OURSELVES TO THIS ONE GREAT ADVENTURE OF BRINGING "PEACE ON EARTH, GOODWILL TO ALL MEN."

Letter from Rev. Gwilym Davies, M.A., President, Welsh National Council, United Nations Association, Aberystwyth, June 13, 1946 (translation)

Heartfelt thanks for transmitting the Welsh Children's Message to the Polish children who are so far from their homes. It is a great encouragement to us to know that, in such a fraught world, at least the children are firm in their belief in friendship and peace between us all.

The account of the work in the school is of great interest to Mrs. Davies and myself. We are charmed by the faces of the little ones - they look so lively and happy - we send our blessings to the school, its pupils and its teachers.

Your letter has raised my spirits and I cannot thank you enough for your thoughtfulness and kindness.

Yours in the bond of peace,

Gwilym Davies

P.S. We were exceedingly grateful for the reply from one of the children.

APPENDIX 8

JANE'S WORK FOR RT/100 FRS among the Jews

When I was accepted by the FRS as a Relief Worker, the Jewish Committee for Relief Abroad, to whom I was well-known, arranged that I could wear their badge (a bronze shield of David) and represent them if I was working in an area where there were Jews and they did not have their own representative.

Accordingly, whilst I was carrying out the clothing distribution at Belsen, the Jewish Army Chaplain of 8th Corps (the Rev L.H.) who was working at Camp 1, heard of me and asked if I could join him since I was the only Jewish civilian relief worker in Belsen.

I spent my days working in Camp 1, which had by then been cleared of the corpses and somewhat tidied up, until the ceremony of the burning of the last hut, which took place on 21st May 1945. My work could best be described as befriending the many internees who were awaiting their transfer to the reception area or hospital. Their circumstances were unbelievably sparse. Trenches had been dug as latrines, but most of them were unscreened, and when I first saw rows of people squatting on them I could not understand what they were doing! The huts had been swept and cleared and there were bunks for sleeping and sitting on, but no other furniture at all. However, the greatest problem was the feeling of absolute loneliness of the internees, in spite of their great numbers. All of them had been bereaved, many, indeed most, had seen their nearest and dearest die, others had lost parents, children, brothers and sisters and friends. I spent much time listening to their stories, there was always someone who could speak English and those who could not believed that I could understand their Yiddish or French or German. It did not matter if I could understand only some of it.

The British military prohibited civilians from writing letters, but since it was of great importance to the internees that they should try to get in touch with their families, the Senior Jewish Chaplain arranged with the Second Army Post Office that Jewish concentration camp internees could send letters to certain countries, via him to Jewish organisations in the countries concerned, and I was able to provide writing materials.

Whilst we were still working at Belsen, I was asked to make a report on a transit camp of 1,135 Polish Jewish men who had been transferred from Belsen to a German military college in nearby Celle, a town a few miles from Belsen. [A copy of Jane's report survives, Ed.]

I was dismayed by the conditions in which they were living. Most of them were still in disgusting, dirty, ragged blue-and-white striped outfits from the concentration camp and wore extremely dilapidated, ill-fitting shoes. Only 250 top garments and 177 pairs of shoes had been delivered there (by UNRRA) and no underwear. The accommodation was totally inadequate and so were their official cooked rations. There were no cooking facilities in the rooms but all the residents were using old tins which they had picked up by the roadside to cook vegetables and meat which they had taken from farms in the vicinity.

Nowadays it is difficult to imagine the circumstances in which these men were living, but at the time it was a hopeful sign that they themselves were taking steps to provide for themselves. An equal number of non-Jewish Poles were living in a different section of the College in similar conditions, it seems. My report to the military authorities at Belsen brought about some improvements, I understand.

On 24th May 1945, with the permission of our Team Leader Lyn, the Red Cross and the military administration, I travelled with a party of 1,127 "stateless" (formally Polish) Jews from Belsen to a camp at Lingen, near the Dutch border, where semi-permanent accommodation had been allocated to them. With the party were two Army Chaplains, both Jewish ministers, one British and one Polish. I was the only civilian relief worker.

British army lorries provided the transport. Each one was allocated 25 passengers although there were seats for only ten; the rest had to stand or sit on the cold metal floors of the lorries. There was heavy driving rain and a strong wind blowing. As the drivers had been instructed to keep the lorries open at the front and back, many of the passengers became sick. Several had only left the camp hospital within the last twenty-four hours and were extremely ill.

The convoy's journey commenced at 12.30 p.m. and took nearly twelve hours to complete its journey, travelling over extremely bad roads. Many of the internees ate the small ration of food distributed for the journey at the lunch-time pause before the journey commenced. There was nothing provided for them to eat on the way.

We arrived at the camp in the dark after 10 p.m. to discover complete chaos. An army camp, it was already housing internees from France, Holland, Italy, Poland, Russia and Yugoslavia. There was a lower camp for our party of "stateless" Jews, which consisted of five large wooden huts for sleeping quarters, similar to those which had been at the Belsen concentration camp. There were no beds, insufficient straw for palliasses, and the only available lighting was provided by the lorry drivers shining their headlights down the corridors of the huts.

An UNRRA food van made an emergency distribution of soup, but as it was dark and there were too few bowls and no cutlery, many people went without. The transport had been received by Major C., the British Military Government Camp Commandant, his deputy, a Captain, a French Army doctor and a Polish liaison officer. They had no idea what ordeals the Belsen internees had endured. It surprised them that the Belsen internees behaved rather differently from the other displaced persons. For instance, they were quite surprised that there were no objections to the requirement that each internee should be sprayed with DDT powder on the first day we were there. I explained that we had all be accustomed to regular daily spraying at Belsen and would miss it if it were no longer required. On the other hand, it was difficult to gain the trust of these internees at first, and they grabbed what food, clothing and blankets were available, indeed everything they could lay their hands on in case they would be left out of any distribution.

Our first two or three days at this camp were still chaotic. Food was in short supply. Bread for breakfast at 11 a.m. was brought in by means of a horse-drawn open cart, which was cleared the moment it appeared. Many people received none at all. The Polish kitchen supplied a late lunch at 5 p.m. and supper at 8.30 p.m. These meals were collected and distributed by block leaders. In addition to the sleeping accommodation in the huts, for which beds and bedding were requisitioned from the local German population within days of our arrival, some huts were allocated for social and recreational activities. The problem was that they were completely unfurnished and unequipped.

On the second day, the Senior Jewish Army Chaplain visited and gave us a talk. He promised that if the residents cleaned up one of the huts and provided the staff, a school could be opened in two days' time for the 86 children in the party. I was rather horrified and shocked, and told him that we had no cleaning materials for this purpose. He said he would find something. The huts were cleaned and scrubbed by the residents, tea-chests were found and planks put across them to make tables, boxes were provided for the children to sit on. The Chaplain returned the next day with paper and pencils he had obtained from the Army, and the school commenced. Never have teachers and children been more thrilled at the opening of a school or more appreciative of its meagre facilities!

Each day the staff of the camp met with the Camp Commandant to discuss the administration of the whole camp. There were 8,000 Russian residents, and it was they who were responsible for the camp's fire precautions. Unfortunately they wrote all the fire protection notices in the Russian language, which few could understand. The Russian liaison officer George, a cheerful person, also spoke only Russian, which made communication difficult. I have always regretted the fact that, when the Russians were due for repatriation, a delegation of Ukrainians, mostly women, came to me and told me they were afraid to return home to the Ukraine which was part of Stalin's Russia. At this time I regarded Russia and Stalin as our allies and friends, and had little understanding of the problem. I advised them to see George and tell him they did not want to be repatriated. I heard later that many who did not wish to be repatriated simply "vanished", but many returned to their homes, and I have often wondered what happened to them. I have since been given to understand that no citizen of the United Nations was to be repatriated against his will, but our relief workers were not informed about this.

Life for my group gradually progressed. They were an amazingly resilient lot, considering their recent suffering. With the constant help of Major L. the Jewish Chaplain and the UNRRA workers, carpentry and shoe-making materials were obtained. A separate kitchen was established, a searcher bureau was set up, and community life began to take shape. But it was not for long, because we were informed that this camp was required for other purposes, and we were to be moved to Diepholz.

The transfer from Lingen to Diepholz, a comparatively short distance, was far easier than that from Belsen to Lingen had been. By now the group had developed some community sense and there were no problems apart from the feeling that we had worked so hard to settle at Lingen that we did not want to move.

The new accommodation was in brick buildings, and less reminiscent of a concentration camp. My own lodgings were some distance from the camp, so I was allocated a motorised pedal cycle, which proved heavy to operate. The school continued its work, and further occupational groups were formed. Lyn visited from Brunswick, bringing Beth to work with me. Although this was an entirely Jewish camp, Kosher food was still not available. The search bureau was co-operating with the Jewish search bureau in London. A drama group and a choir were established. After nearly two weeks we were informed that a Jewish Relief Team would be coming from London, and that I should rejoin our team in Brunswick.

I had made many friends in this group, and was sorry to leave. A petition signed by most of the group asked that I should remain with them. If I was to continue to be a member of the FRS Team, this was not possible, and I left.

The end of this story is rather sad. The group was returned to Belsen, because the authorities decided that the Belsen camp hospital and residential area were to be handed over to the care of the British Jewish Committee for Relief Abroad, who were to be responsible for all residents until they were transferred to countries willing to receive them. Thus the remainder of my group were returned to Belsen to wait with all the others. Belsen became a "model" camp but it was never a home.

When Lyn came to fetch me from Diepholz, she told me I should take some leave before I started work in Brunswick. I went with Joyce to Bad Harzburg for a week's leave. I had not wanted to go, but it was a wise decision and I returned refreshed. While at Bad Harzburg I looked up the grandmother of a little half-Jewish German boy whom my sister had fostered in London from 1938, when he was four. In this way his life had probably been saved, for the little boy's father and the grandfather had died at the time of "Kristallnacht". As we were waiting in the sitting-room for the grandmother to be fetched, I was thrilled to see a photograph of my sister and the little boy on top of the piano. The old lady had taught herself English during the war, and was able to get in touch with her daughter-in-law and the little boy through my visit to her.

When I first started work in Brunswick, I was attached to a different Polish displaced persons camp from the Gypsy Camp at which many of the team were now working. I liaised with a Polish Army captain who had been a prisoner-of-war, who was in charge. I was able to establish social activities, a search bureau, the distribution of such items as razor blades and baby food. All things considered, this camp was well-administered.

In my spare time I went in to the centre of Brunswick, where I was surprised to find that the Jewish Hospitality Committee had established a services' club for British servicemen of all denominations which was administered by Jewish workers. There were bars and cafes for officers, NCO's and other ranks. On Friday nights the local Jewish Army chaplains conducted eve of Sabbath services in turn, and afterwards held informal discussions with those who attended. I attended these services and discussions regularly.

This led to other developments. By this time, in Brunswick and the surrounding area, a few scores of Jews, survivors of the concentration camps or those who had managed to remain in hiding, had taken over some vacant apartments and established a near-normal existence. They had to register in the local community house (gemeindehaus) to obtain identity cards and ration books. They set up an office there to search for their families. They visited the local displaced persons camps to look for their friends, but not many of them lived there, preferring their independence. I befriended many of these people.

The Jewish Services Club allowed me to invite some of these people into the Centre for Sabbath (Saturday) gatherings. They also made space available for Jewish weddings to be held (under a canopy, the chuppah), conducted by the Polish rabbi. On these occasions there was much dancing and singing, also weeping, for the release of tension on these occasions was immense.

On the occasion of Jewish High Holy days (New Year and the Day of Atonement) the Club made a room available for services, and many people came in from the surrounding area to stay for the twenty-four hours of each service.

The problem was to find accommodation. I asked our Military Government Major W., who by this time had come to know our team and it worked rather well, if I could borrow a hundred army beds for the ten days. At first he seemed outraged at the suggestion, and bawled "No! No!, Jane, a thousand times No!". As I turned to leave his office, he asked; "What did you want me to say?". When I said "Yes!" he relented, and said "Alright, but not for more than ten days". You see, our relations with the military were really quite satisfactory!

Searching for the family and friends of these Jewish people was most rewarding. Sometimes I was successful; it was however a very slow process, and the results sometimes did not come through till after I had left. [Jane went to Poland and worked there for a while, travelling on one of the transports which we arranged for repatriation. Beth preceded her to undertake welfare work in Poland after her time in Brunswick: Ed.]

I was also able to start the process of applications for visas for those who wished to enter various European countries, also Israel (then Palestine) and the USA. There was one couple in whom I took the greatest interest. They had both been for a comparatively short time in Auschwitz, and their arms bore those tattoo-ed numbers to prove it. They were married by the Polish rabbi at the Service's centre. They emigrated to Israel whilst I was in Poland. He became a taxi-driver and sent me a case of oranges from his first week's wages. She wanted to study, and eventually they emigrated to Toronto - and this clever girl, whose early education was ended by her arrest and internment, became a well-known scientist and lecturer at Toronto University. One is bound to reflect how many clever and admirable people's lives were ended before they had really begun!

APPENDIX 9

Assembly Centre 296 - RT100/FRS

Various Facts and Statistics about "Gypsy Camp"

FIRST FRS MEMBER (Hugh J.) entered the camp called 'GYPSY" by the American forces on Friday, 13th July 1945, when it was still occupied by the Americans.

Planning and preparation, hampered by the fact that we were not allowed to bring in any labour, continued until July 25th, when the Americans left at 0900hrs and the Polish guard under Sgt. Malinski came in.

The first Polish residents, 91 in number, arrived the same afternoon at 1600 hrs; by the next Wednesday August 1st we had 741 residents.

The first House Commandants Conference took place on 30th July.

The school was planned at the Conference on August 2nd and preparations started immediately; the school was opened on August 21st.

Total Receptions from July 25th to 3rd May 1946   5931
Total Departures   4096

Transports to Poland

14.10.1945 (24 hrs notice)   797
16.11.1945   374
14.12.1945   118

22. 2.1946	129
16. 3.1946	450
10. 4.1946	687
2. 5.1946	259

Total 2814

plus 19. 9.1945 (transfer of single men to Osnabruck)   266

Highest population of camp - 29.12.1945   3030

Displaced Persons in area taken over 17.11.1945 handed over to 135 GIS 26. 1.1946	237
Births	119
Deaths (including 2 fatal accidents)	11
Residents sent to Hospital	308
Number of Camps evacuated into our Centre	50

Residents received from 42 German towns and cities and 11 villages, also from Schleswig-Holstein, the Dutch border, Berlin, Brussels, and from Austria and Poland itself.